The Story of Leather

(Sara Ware Bassett)

CHAPTER I

THE THUNDERBOLT

Peter Coddington sat in the afternoon sunshine on the steps of his big colonial home looking absently out over the circular drive, and the quaint terraced garden, to the red-tiled roof of the garage beyond. But he was not thinking of the garage; he could not, in fact, even have told you the color of its vivid tiling. No! He had far more important things to think of than that--disquieting things which worried him and made him very unhappy. For about the twentieth time he took from his pocket his school report and ran his eye down the column of figures written upon the white card. He did not read because the reading gave him pleasure. Neither was the bit of pasteboard white any more. Instead it was thumbed and worn at the corners until it had gradually assumed a dismal grayish hue--a color quite in harmony with Peter's own mood.

Peter really did not need to look at the report at all, for already he could close his eyes and see before him in glaring type:

Algebra 40 History 20 Latin 30 French 30 Drawing 25

What a horrible fascination there was in those marks! He found himself repeating them aloud to impress upon his mind the fact that they actually were true. But what was far more tragic than these testimonials of defeat was a foot-note written in red ink in the well-known hand of Mr. Christopher, the principal of the school. It read:

"In consequence of Peter Coddington's poor scholarship and unsatisfactory deportment it is against the rules of the Milburn High School that he retain any position in school athletics until such time as both his studies and his conduct reach the standard required by the school authorities."

It was that single sentence that made Peter's face so grave. The marks alone were bad enough. He was heartily ashamed of them because he knew that if he had studied even a reasonable amount of time he could easily have passed in every subject. It was by no means difficult work for a boy of his ability. But to be put off the ball team! Why, it was on his pitching that the whole Milburn school was pinning its faith in the coming game against Leighton Academy. "Peter will save the day!" the fellows had declared. What would they say when they discovered that their hero was to be dropped from the team--that he had not passed one of the freshman examinations?

Half the pride and glory of the freshman class centered about Peter. Throughout the grammar school he had made a wonderful record in athletics; his unerring drop kick had won him fame at football long before he was out of the sixth grade, and he could pitch a ball with a speed and curve almost professional in its nicety. "Wait until Peter Coddington gets into the high school!" had been the cry. "Milburn can then wipe up the ground with every school within reach." As Peter had never been much of a student the gate of this temple of learning had been difficult to reach; but at last the day came when he managed to squeak inside the coveted portals where all the honors promised him were at once laid at his feet. He became a member of the football eleven, pitcher on the freshman nine, president of his class. Friends swarmed about him, for he had a pleasant way of greeting everybody, he treated generously, and he had a winsome little chuckle that spread merriment wherever he went.

None of these qualities, however, helped his poor scholarship, which he jauntily excused by explaining to his father at the end of the first quarter that he had not really got into the game yet. In consequence Mr. Coddington listened and was patient. When the mid-year record dropped even lower Peter's argument was that it took time to adjust one's self to novel conditions. But as spring brought no improvement Mr. Coddington, a man of few words, remarked severely: "I will give you one more chance, son."

The list of figures in Peter's hand were the fruit of that chance.

Peter had a wholesome awe of his father. He was not a man to be bamboozled. On the contrary Mr. Coddington was a keen, direct person who came straight to a point in a few terse sentences; predominant in his character was an unflinching sense of justice which was, however, fortunately tempered with enough kindness to make a misdoer mortified but never afraid in his presence. Peter admired his father tremendously and if for one reason more than another because he was so "square." Never during all the span of the lad's fifteen years could he recall a single instance when Mr. Coddington had broken his word. It was this knowledge that made Peter so uncomfortable as he glanced once more at the bedraggled report card. What had his father meant by saying he would grant him one more chance?

The boy wished now that he had considered the matter in a more serious light. He had known all along that his marks were dropping behind, and every morning he had vaguely resolved to make a spurt that day so that when examination time came he might cross the tape neck and neck with if not in advance of the other fellows. The promised spurt, however, had not been made. Instead he had drifted along, studying only enough to keep his head above water and putting all his zeal into tennis or baseball until the present climax with its direful calamity had been reached.

Unquestionably it was perfectly fair that he should forfeit his place on the team. All the boys knew the rule of the school. But somehow it did not seem *real*. When a fellow could kick a goal and pitch a ball as he could something must surely intervene to prevent such a fate. Nothing dreadful had ever happened to Peter before. It was not likely, he argued optimistically, that it could happen now. Considerably cheered by this logic he slipped his grimy report into its still more grimy envelope and began to whistle. Buoyed up by comfortable reveries he whistled fully five minutes, when the tune came to an abrupt end. A step on the gravel had arrested it. Looking around Peter saw his father coming along the drive toward him.

"Not at the game to-day, Peter?" exclaimed the elder man in surprise.

"No, sir."

"How is that?"

"I did not feel like going, Father."

"Not feel like going! Why, that's something new for you. You're not sick?"

Peter was conscious of a swift scrutiny.

"I'm worried about something," he blurted out.

"I'm sorry to hear that, my boy. What is the trouble? Grass stains on your new white tennis flannels?"

Peter shook his head in reply to the smiling question.

"It is a real trouble this time," he answered.

Silently he drew from his pocket the crumpled envelope which he handed to his father. As Mr. Coddington took out the card and scanned it rapidly the quizzical expression that had lighted his face gave way to a frown of displeasure.

"Well?" he questioned.

"I'm mighty sorry, Father," began Peter. "You see I kept thinking I would make up my work before the exams came; but somehow I have been hustling more for the baseball championship than----"

A curt question cut short further apologies:

"Your studies have not been too difficult for you, then?"

"Oh, no. I can easily make them up with a tutor," was the eager response. "I guess if you ask Mr. Christopher he will let me take the examinations over again before school closes and the next time----"

"There is to be no next time," put in his father quietly.

Peter stared.

"Wh-a-t--do--you mean, sir?"

"You will see."

Without another word the older man turned away. Peter saw him walk to the garage, and a few moments later the motor-car shot past, spun down the drive, and the music of its siren horn announced that it was turning into the street. Where had his father gone so suddenly?

He had but just come home, and it was never his custom to dash off in such an abrupt fashion. It was easy to see that he was annoyed about the school report. That was not strange--of course he would be. Peter was himself. But at least Mr. Coddington had not lost his place as pitcher of a ball team, and since he hadn't there seemed to be no reason why he should be so cut up. Then an inspiration came to the boy. Perhaps his father had gone to demand that Mr. Christopher take his son back on the nine. Ah, that must be it! His father was much interested in athletics Peter knew, and when in college had pulled the winning shell to a spectacular victory for his Alma Mater. His father would never stand by and see the star pitcher of the Milburn High School swept off the team just because of a few failures in Latin, algebra, and other such rubbish.

Peter drew a sigh of relief.

Yes, his fortunate star would rise again; he was confident of it. All would yet be well. He would tutor up for the examinations, pass them gloriously, and win back his place on the team. None of the fellows need be the wiser. His father would fix it up--nay, he probably was fixing it up at this very moment.

Until dusk Peter waited anxiously for the sound of the motor's return.

It was nearly seven when over the gravel rolled the heavy rubber-tired wheels that announced Mr. Coddington's arrival. The boy sat in precisely the spot where his father had left him and after alighting from the car the elder man made his way toward the motionless figure sitting so still in the June twilight.

"I have been to see Mr. Christopher," began Mr. Coddington when he came within speaking distance, "and have made all the arrangements for your future career."

Eagerly Peter looked up.

"I'm going back on the team?" he cried joyously.

"You are going to work!" was the sharp retort.

"What!"

"I have been very busy during the last two hours," continued Mr. Coddington. "I have got for you the first, last, and only job I shall ever get. It is up to you now."

"But I don't understand," protested Peter, aghast.

"Why not? It is not a difficult thing to comprehend. You have fooled away your days and my money long enough. Life is a serious business--not a game. It is time you took it in earnest. To-morrow morning at eight o'clock you are going to work, and you must make good at the position I've found for you, or you will lose your place. If you do I shall not lift a finger to help you to find another."

A great lump rose in Peter's throat but he managed to choke it back.

"Where am I going?" he gasped when he was able to speak.

"To the tannery," was the laconic reply.

If the clouds had fallen or the earth opened Peter could not have been more astounded.

The tannery!

Of course he knew his father owned the vast tanneries to the west of the town, for that was the reason the Coddingtons lived at Milburn instead of migrating to the near-by city, as had so many of their prosperous neighbors; but beyond the fact that it was the tanneries which indirectly provided him with tennis racquets, skates, bicycles, motor-cars, and spending money Peter knew nothing about them. They were red brick buildings covering a wide area, and from their doors at noon and night hundreds of workmen with lunch-boxes and newspaper bundles poured out into the streets. Peter never spoke of the tanneries. Even when, on the highway, he encountered the heavy carts laden with hides and marked "H. M. Coddington, Leather," he always looked the other way and hurried past as fast as he could. Occasionally in hot weather when the wind was in a certain quarter and brought a faint odor from the beamhouses into the fashionable part of the town where Peter lived their neighbors complained, and the boy always felt with a vague sense of mortification that everybody blamed him and his family for the annoyance. Sometimes this breath of damp, steamy leather even forced itself in at the windows of the Coddington library and mingled shamelessly with the rich hangings and paintings that furnished it. Peter always resented the intrusion. How dare it follow them there!

Mr. Coddington, on the other hand, although not reveling in the unpleasant tannery smells, had a sincere respect for the industry which furnished him his living, not only because it enabled him to provide his family with a luxurious home, but also because he regarded it as a life-work that was well worth the doing. Was he not giving to the world a necessity which it could not do without? It was a self-respecting trade. Therefore why should he not feel there was dignity in the long buildings with their whirring wheels, their hundreds of busy workmen, and their ponderous green trucks which, loaded with skins, ever rumbled back and forth through the main street? His pride was the more justifiable since alone, and aided only by his brain and his perseverance, he himself had built up this mighty industry which had become the chief support of the flourishing little New England town. Milburn, in fact, had grown up around the business that he had founded. From the lowest rung of the ladder he had worked his way up to the highest. The climb had been no easy one. On the contrary it had been hard work. How could he help but feel a pride--nay, an affection, even, for the great throbbing world of labor which he had created, and which furnished thousands of people with homes, food and clothing!

Since this was his point of view it naturally was impossible for him to appreciate the horror that his words brought to the boy who sat on the steps beside him. Peter knew his father too well to offer protest at the judgment that his own misdeeds had brought. It was a perfectly fair retribution. Moreover, he had been warned--Peter clearly recalled the fact now. But he had rushed blindly on, not heeding the warning.

"The tannery?" he at last repeated aloud.

"Yes. That is where I began, Peter, and it won't hurt you to do the same."

"Shan't I go back to school at all?"

"Not for the present."

"And the school team----"

"It must get on without you as best it may."

Peter fought to keep back the tears.

"Will everybody know?" he faltered after a pause.

"No. I simply told Mr. Christopher that I had decided to take you out of school. He knows nothing more, nor does any one else. Now, Peter, I do not wish you to take this as a punishment." Stooping, Mr. Coddington put his hand kindly on the lad's shoulder. "In so far as it is the consequence of misspent, wasted time it is, to be sure, a punishment; none of us can escape the direct results of our own actions. In another sense, however, it is merely a fresh opportunity--a chance to substitute success for failure, to make good at a different kind of work. It is in this light that you must try and regard it, son. I want to make a man of you if I can. I must make a man of you. You are the only child I have, and if I stand by and allow you to make a fizzle of your life I shall be quite as much to blame as you. Remember that unhappy as you are this affair is costing me something, too."

There was a break in Mr. Coddington's voice.

As the boy raised his head and looked into the face bending over him he read in it an expression quite new--a softness and sympathy that he had never before caught in the gray eyes which, but a moment previous, had regarded him so sternly.

As a result when Peter answered much of the bitterness had crept out of his tone.

"I suppose all the men at the factory will have to know who I am," he reflected.

"I'm afraid so. I see no way that that can be avoided," assented his father.

"I hate to have them. They will all be grinning over the knowledge that I was put into the factories because I flunked at school. Isn't there any way to prevent their knowing? Couldn't I take another name when I go into the tannery and let them think I am somebody else?"

Mr. Coddington mused a few seconds before answering.

"Why, yes," he replied meditatively, "I suppose it could be done. Nobody knows you at the works, so there would be no danger of your being recognized. My plan to send you there I have kept to myself. You could easily enter under some other name if you chose. You must consider, however, that if you decide to go in simply as an ordinary boy I shall not be able to help you much; nor can you expect to be favored in any way by the men. You would have to stand on your own feet and take your own chances." Again Mr. Coddington ruminated. "That might not be a bad idea, either," he observed, half aloud.

"Oh, I would so much rather take another name, Father," pleaded Peter.

But Mr. Coddington did not heed the interruption; he was still thinking.

"I do not mean to stand behind you after you are in the tannery, anyway," he went on. "In every department there is a foreman to whom you will be accountable--not to me. Nor must you come running home and here report every real or fancied injustice. So far as business goes I am the president of the company and you are simply a boy in my employ. Out of working hours we will be father and son and will enjoy our drives, walks, and reading together just as we have in the past. One rule, however, must be strictly adhered to--we will not talk shop."

"I understand, sir," nodded Peter.

"Now just a last word," concluded Mr. Coddington. "To-morrow morning you must be prompt at the works. Eight o'clock is the hour you are to present yourself and that does not mean before eight or after eight; it means on the stroke of eight. You will carry a luncheon which your mother will see is put up for you. You are to hand to Mr. Tyler, the superintendent of Factory 1, a card bearing my signature and you are to say to him that you are the boy I telephoned him about. He does not know who you are, but he understands that I am interested in you and he will start you in wherever he thinks best. On the card I shall write your name--and by the by"--a smile flitted over Mr. Coddington's face--"what is your name to be?"

Peter hesitated; then his lips curved into a faint reflection of his father's merriment.

"I think I will enter the tannery as Peter Strong," he answered.

CHAPTER II

PETER WINS ANOTHER NAME

The next morning when, at half-past six, the small alarm clock at his bedside shot off with metallic clangor Peter raised himself drowsily on his elbow and glanced about. What had happened? What was all this jangling about? In a second more, however, he recollected. This was the day when school, fun, and friends were to be left behind, and when he was to set forth into a new world. He was going to work! Slowly, unwillingly, with a vague sinking at heart, he dragged himself to his feet and listened. It was very still. All the world appeared to have stopped and the only being alive in the great universe seemed to be himself. He prepared to dress. Half automatically he turned on the shower-bath. The chill of the cold water sent a tingle over him and quickened his awakening faculties. Pulling on his clothes he crept down over the stairs. It was bad enough to have to get up at this unearthly hour himself; he at least need not disturb the rest of the household. Of course his father would get up and start him off.

But to Peter's surprise nothing of this sort happened. Instead he sat down alone in the big dining-room to a forlorn breakfast, at the conclusion of which the waitress laid on the table beside him a carefully packed lunch-box. Now Peter detested taking a lunch. Whenever he went with his parents on motor trips or train journeys the family always stopped at hotels for their meals or patronized the dining-cars. It seemed such a vulgar thing to open a box and in the gaze of lookers on devour one's food out of it. Accordingly he eyed the lunch-box with disdain, mentally arguing that although he must, out of gratitude to his mother's thoughtfulness, carry it, he certainly should not open it. He would far rather go hungry than eat a lunch from a box!

On the porch still another unpleasant feature of this going to work greeted him. No motor-car, panting like a hound on the leash, stood waiting to carry him to the factory. Evidently his father had made no provision for him to get to the tannery. He must walk! So entirely unforeseen was this development that the boy stood a moment irresolute. It was a good mile to the tan yards; he had had no notion of walking, and there was now but scant time in which to cover the distance. Perhaps his father had forgotten to order the car. Peter had half a mind not to go. After all what difference would it make whether he went to-day or to-morrow? In fact, why wasn't it better to delay until to-morrow when he could be sure of not being late? He vacillated uneasily. Then the thought of what his father would say when he came down to breakfast and found that his son had not gone decided Peter.

Down two steps at a time he dashed and set out over the gravel drive with the even jog of a track sprinter. On he went. Running in the June sunshine was hot work; nevertheless, hat in hand, he kept up the pace. He must be there promptly at eight, his father had told him. He could feel tiny streams of perspiration trickling down his back, and he sensed that his collar was wilting into a limp band of flimsy linen. Still he ran on. Eight was just on the stroke when he presented himself at the office of Factory 1.

A stout man bending over a ledger at a desk near the door eyed the panting lad with disapproval.

"What do you want?" he demanded sharply. "Boys are not admitted in this office."

"I want to see Mr. Tyler," gasped Peter.

"Well, you can't," the bookkeeper responded acidly. "He's busy. If you are wanting a job I can tell you right now that there are none to be had. We have more boys already than we know what to do with. You better not wait. It won't do any good."

"But I must see Mr. Tyler," persisted Peter. "My fa---- I was told to give him this card."

"Why didn't you say you had a card in the first place?" was the gruff question. "Give it here. You can sit down on that bench and wait."

As the accountant held out his hand Peter delivered up the card.

"Peter Strong--hump!" read the bookkeeper. "Sent by--oh, you're sent by Mr. Coddington, are you? Some relative of his, perhaps."

"Mr. Coddington said I was to present the card to Mr. Tyler," Peter answered, ignoring the implied query.

"He shall have it right away, Strong. You'll excuse my brusqueness. I did not understand that you were sent here. We have so many young boys applying for work that we have to pack them off in short order," explained the man glibly.

It was evident that he was not a little discomfited at the chill reception he had accorded Peter, for he anxiously continued to reiterate excuses and apologies. Fortunately in the midst of his explanations an electric bell beside his desk rang and cut him short.

"That is Mr. Tyler now," he murmured. "I'll take in your card right away."

Peter watched him as he hurried down the center of the long room and disappeared into a little glass cage in the corner.

It was an oblong room in which reigned the din of typewriters. Over against the farther wall a dozen or more men were bending so intently over heavy, leather-bound ledgers that it seemed as if they must have sat in that exact spot from the beginning of the world, adding, adding, adding! Vacantly the lad's eye wandered along to the space just opposite him where, framed in neat oak, hung a printed notice headed: "Labor Laws of the State of Massachusetts." For the want of a better amusement Peter sauntered over and began to read. The length of the working day, he gathered, was ten hours except for boys under sixteen, whom the law forbade working longer than eight hours. A smile passed over the lad's face. Eight hours was surely long enough--from eight until twelve, and from one until five. What if he had been sixteen instead of fifteen, and been forced to get to the tannery at seven o'clock in the morning and work until six at night! There must be boys who did. For the first time in his life Peter was thankful that he was no older.

Just at this moment he saw the bookkeeper returning.

"If you please, Strong," said the older man with a deference that contrasted markedly with his former greeting, "will you step this way? Mr. Tyler is expecting you."

Peter followed through the central aisle of the long room and entered the small, glass-enclosed space where a man surrounded by a chaos of papers and letters was sitting at a roll-top desk.

"This, Mr. Tyler, is young Strong," announced the bookkeeper to the superintendent.

"I am glad to see you, Strong."

So sharply did his eye sweep over Peter that the boy trembled lest this oracle suddenly announce:

"I know all about you. Your name is not Strong at all. You are Peter Coddington, and you have been sent to the mill because you flunked your examinations."

Nothing of the sort happened, however. The superintendent merely remarked with a nod: "That will do, Carter. You may go."

Peter heard the latch click as Mr. Carter went out.

"Well, young man, so you want a job in the tannery?" were Mr. Tyler's next words.

"Yes, sir."

"Mr. Coddington telephoned me about you. He told me that you are entirely inexperienced and with no knowledge of the business. I should say the only thing for you to do is to begin at the very bottom of the ladder, if you want to make anything of yourself."

"I suppose so, sir."

The superintendent tilted back in his chair and carefully studied the lad before him.

"You look able-bodied."

"Oh, yes, sir."

"Not afraid of work?"

Peter hesitated.

"I don't mind working if I like what I'm doing, sir," he replied with naive truthfulness.

It was obvious that the honest reply pleased Mr. Tyler.

"I guess that is the way with many of us, Strong," he laughed. "But if you are to have a position here you will have to stick at your work whether you like it or not."

"I mean to try to."

"That's the proper spirit. You are not afraid of getting your hands dirty?"

Peter laughed contemptuously. Later he remembered that laugh and smiled grimly at his own ignorance.

Mr. Tyler seemed satisfied.

"Well, I can set you to work right away unloading skins," he said. "We are short-handed and can use a boy to advantage. Are you over sixteen?"

"No, sir, I am fifteen."

"That's bad. I don't like to take these eight-hour boys. The time we want workmen most is in the early morning and at closing time. Those are the very hours you under-age fellows are not here. However, since you have come at Mr. Coddington's recommendation we'll have to get on without you the best way we can. Strong, your name is! Do you know Mr. Coddington personally?"

"I've known him all my life," was the reply.

"Then you know an honest, upright gentleman," declared Mr. Tyler warmly. "His friendship is well worth having and a possession to be proud of. Take care you do not disappoint him."

"I do not mean to disappoint him," was Peter's quick reply. "He told me, though, that after he got me the place he should not do anything more for me. I've got to make good myself. He's the president of the company and I am just a boy in the works."

Unconsciously the lad repeated his father's very words.

"That's right. That's the way to go at it," the superintendent assented cordially. "It is very kind of Mr. Coddington to bother his head about you at all, for he is such a busy man that he has more things to remember in a day than most of the rest of us have ever thought of in all our lives. After you once get in here he, of course, can't take the time to follow you up. Having done you the favor of giving you a start he will drop you from his mind. You cannot expect anything else and I am glad you have common sense enough to see it."

At the thought of his father "dropping him from his mind" Peter smiled inwardly. Of course Mr. Tyler could not see the smile, and even if he had he would not have understood it. As it was he now cut short the interview by touching a bell at his elbow in response to which a messenger appeared.

"Take this boy down to the yard, Johnson," he said. "Introduce him to Carmachel and tell him he is to help unload skins. His name is Strong. Good luck to you, young man. Remember the world is a large place and there are plenty of fine positions waiting for the men who prove themselves big enough to fill them."

Peter took the superintendent's hand but he forgot to answer. Somehow Mr. Tyler's words awakened a train of thoughts which were so entirely new that he could not immediately drive them from his mind. So the great universe of work demanded that you should fill your position, not rattle round in it! The mere fact that one had a rich father did not help much then after all. It might aid you in keeping your job, to be sure, but it could not aid you in doing it. Evidently at the Coddington tanneries there were plenty of men ready to take your chance if you were not smart enough to hold on to it yourself. Peter decided that it behooved him to "hustle." It was a novel sensation to feel this spur to action.

As he thus philosophized he was following his guide, who now turned down a flight of steep steps into a yard slippery with black mud and deeply rutted by the wheels of heavy wagons. A double track with a row of freight cars flanked the building opposite, and from these cars a group of men were unloading bundles of skins and tossing them on the platform. The men were dressed in faded jumpers and overalls and some of them wore rubber aprons.

They glanced up an instant as Peter drew near.

"Carmachel," called the man who was showing the way, "this young fellow is to help at unloading and later, the boss says, he is to watch you fellows sort skins. He is a green lad and," added the messenger with a grin of enjoyment at some joke that Peter did not at all comprehend, "his name is Strong."

Carmachel, a grizzled Irishman, looked up--a twinkle in his eye.

"It's Strong he'll have to be if he is to work here," he answered with a chuckle in which the others joined. "I say, young one," he continued kindly, "you're not figuring on unloading skins in those clothes, are you?"

"I was," replied Peter, nodding.

"Well, before you begin, you better have another think. It will be the end of your glad rags. It's truth I'm tellin' you. Step inside the doorway and wriggle yourself into those brown jeans you'll see hangin' there."

Peter went in.

He took down the jeans from a peg behind the door. The clothes were dirty, sticky with salt, and in them lingered a loathsome aroma of wet hides. Instinctively he shrank from touching them. Then, gritting his teeth, he put them on. This he did more out of appreciation for the rough kindliness of the old Irishman than because he feared to injure his clothes; his father would give him plenty more suits if that one was spoiled.

When he went out on the platform Carmachel eyed him.

"That's more like it," he said. "Now get busy. We want to pull these cars out of the yard by noon. Step lively."

Peter crossed the wet, slippery platform to the car where the other men were working. The skins were folded neatly and tied with stout cord. He lifted the bundle nearest at hand, then dropped it. It was solid, sticky, and damp.

"They're wet!" he exclaimed.

"For certain they're wet!" roared the Irishman with a noisy guffaw. "You're as green as the skins themselves--greener, for you are not even salted."

The gang on the platform shouted at the joke.

Peter's anger rose, but he struggled to take their chaffing in good part.

"You see, I don't know a thing about all this business," confessed he, frankly. "You fellows who do will have to tell me."

The answer struck the right note with the men.

"How could you be expected to know, sonny?" called a red-faced Swede kindly. "Every boy who comes into the tannery has to learn."

"Pitch a few skins out of the car, lad, while I tell you some things," broke in Carmachel. "You are unloading calfskins; that's the only kind we tan at Factory 1. Over at Factory 2 they tan sheepskins, and at Factory 3 cowhides. In each of these factories the skins are treated and prepared for the trade quite differently, as you will learn by and by if you have the chance to go through the other buildings. These calfskins that we are unloading came from the Chicago slaughter-houses, where as soon as they were taken off the animals they were salted; folded with the head, tail, and small parts inside; tied in bales such as you see; and shipped. They are what we call green-salted. We also get green-salted skins from the abattoirs of the city of Paris, and from lots of other places, too. Sometimes, though, skins are salted green and are then dried like those you saw piled up in the shed; those we call dry-salted. They came from Norway, Sweden, and South America. Then we have dry hides which are dried without being salted at all. Remember now--green-salted, dry-salted, and dry."

Peter repeated the terms.

At the same time he did his share in tossing the heavy bales of moist skins to the platform. It was strenuous work. Before an hour was up his back and arms ached with the unaccustomed exercise. Tennis and football were as nothing to this! Still he went on uncomplainingly. His unflagging energy appealed to the men.

"Knock off, lad, and rest a bit," called Carmachel at last. "You're not toughened to this job as we are. It's a precious lame back you'll have to-morrow if you keep at it like this the first time."

Gratefully Peter straightened up and took a long breath. Then he glanced at his hands.

"You'll be losing your gentlemanly white hands, if that's what's worrying you," grinned Carmachel, reading his thoughts with disconcerting keenness.

"Oh, I'm not afraid of my hands," replied Peter, mortified at being detected in such a foolish reflection. "I was just thinking that they are beginning to look the part."

"If you are aiming to work up through the tannery they'll likely look the part more by the time you've got a few coats of lime and blacking on them," was Carmachel's dry response. "Now we'll let the others finish this work. You come inside and you shall have a new job. You've done enough unloading for your first day."

Obediently Peter followed into the shed, where other men were busy cutting the cords from round the skins, looking them over, and tossing some into one pile and some into another.

"These fellows that you see are sorting the calfskins according to their weight," explained Carmachel. "We get them flat--by that I mean that when the bales are made up all sizes and qualities of skins are tied in together. These men put the fine, heavy ones in one pile, the medium weight in another, the light weight in another, the imperfect ones in another, and so on."

"I do not see how they can tell so quickly," said Peter.

"They couldn't if they hadn't done it a good many times before. They are skilled men. Watch them. It does not take them many minutes to determine the value of a skin."

"And what are those other men doing?" Peter questioned, pointing to a group of workmen who were engaged in swiftly cutting off parts of the skins with long knives.

"Oh, they are taking off the heads and other good-for-nothing parts which are sold for glue stock. Nothing is wasted in a tannery, let me tell you! After the skins leave this room they will be sent to the beamhouse, where they will be soaked in water until all the dirt and salt is out of them. Usually this takes from twenty-four to forty-eight hours."

"What's the beamhouse?" was Peter's query.

"The beamhouse? I'll not be telling you. 'Twould be a sin to spoil your first sight of it." Carmachel shook his head. "No, young one, I'll tell you nothing of the beamhouse. You'll find out in time. There's many a pleasant spot awaiting you in this tannery."

A general snicker went around.

Again Peter did not understand.

"Now," declared Carmachel briskly, "you have idled long enough. Take that knife and go to cutting the twine from those bales of skins."

At this task the boy worked faithfully until the noon whistle blew. At its first blast all the men dropped what they were doing and Peter, who did the same, followed them into a washroom, where he scoured his hands with sand soap. Somehow he did not feel as scornful toward his box of lunch as he had when he had tucked it under his arm in the early morning. Instead he made his way out into the vacant field opposite where he saw the men congregating, and sitting down in the shade of one of the factories, lifted the tin cover with keenest anticipation. How good it seemed to rest, and how faint he was! He devoured the food hurriedly with the quick greed of hunger. He then glanced about him. Some boys and men were sauntering with bat and ball out into the open field. Apparently a noontide game was a part of the daily program, for two nines were quickly organized and a match was under way in the twinkling of an eye. The other workmen drew near to watch the play and so did Peter. He wondered how any one could summon energy enough to toss a ball. They couldn't be as tired as he was! The game began. Before it had proceeded beyond the first inning it was obvious that the teams were unevenly matched.

[Illustration: A MATCH WAS UNDER WAY]

"It's the sheepskins against the calfskins--Factory 1 against Factory 2," explained a man at his elbow. "Factory 1 could do 'em if we had a decent pitcher. O'Brien, who is pitching, isn't much even when he's in the best of trim; to-day he happens to have a sprained finger, so he's worse than usual."

Instantly Peter was alert. Wasn't he Factory 1? He forgot his fatigue--forgot everything except how it felt to pitch when one had a sprained finger.

"I can pitch a ball," he ventured modestly.

"Can you then? O'Brien!" bawled the man. "Here's a lad who says he can pitch. Give him a try, won't you?"

Despite aching muscles and tired back Peter suddenly found himself on the diamond with the ball in his hands. It was the first familiar experience that had come to him that day. His blood warmed. He sent a twirler over the plate and was greeted by a roar from the Factory 1 men. The ball dropped with a smack into the hands of the catcher.

Peter tried another.

He pitched a third.

Vainly the man at the bat tried to hit them.

"Three strikes and out!" called the umpire.

The crowd cheered.

On went the game.

"Who's pitching?" asked one man of another.

Nobody knew.

"Carmachel says his name is Strong," some one at last informed the workmen.

"Hurrah for little Strong!" yelled a big Swede.

"Three cheers for the Little Giant!" piped a shrill voice.

On every hand the cry was taken up.

"Three cheers for the Little Giant!"

Then suddenly the one o'clock whistle sounded. Peter came back to the realities of life. He dropped his gloves. Already, as if the earth had opened, players and audience had vanished. In through the waiting doors of the tanneries filed the men. But Peter Coddington had won a place for himself, and with it a new name. Henceforth throughout the works he was known as "The Little Giant."

CHAPTER III

A NEW FRIEND

For a week Peter worked patiently cutting ropes from freshly received shipments of skins, trimming the skins, and learning to sort them. Every night he went home exhausted after his day's work. Sometimes it was hard to realize that he was the same boy who, but a short time before, had jauntily sauntered out to play tennis every evening with his classmates. He couldn't have played tennis now had he tried, and he was not sorry when the rumor reached him that it was commonly reported at the high school that he had been sent away to a distant military academy. So that was the reason why the fellows had not hunted him up! Perhaps it was just as well. It saved many embarrassing questions, and he was much too worn out when night came to do anything but fall into his bed. Still he did not complain of his fatigue. He was too proud to do that. Moreover had he not brought the entire situation upon himself? He would swallow his medicine in silence.

But he knew from his mother's troubled questions; from her unusual care that his luncheon be tempting and nourishing; from the solicitous gaze she fixed on him that the present ordeal worried her not a little. Once he overheard her say to his father: "The boy isn't strong enough to stand it! He will be ill."

"Don't have any anxiety about Peter," was the retort. "The young scoundrel finds energy enough, I hear, to play ball with the men every noon time. He is the star pitcher of Factory 1." A chuckle came from the older man. "It is something of a joke, too," he continued, "for I thought I had put him beyond all possible range of a bat and ball. Don't fret any more about him. Let him alone. He is showing more pluck than I dreamed he possessed."

"But suppose he should overdo."

"He won't overdo."

And the prediction was true. Tired as he was every night Peter awoke in the morning entirely refreshed. The lameness of back and muscles soon wore away. At the end of the week, when he received his first pay envelope, no boy in the wide world ever felt as rich as he. Six dollars! Six dollars of his very own! To be sure his father had often given him twice that amount; but receiving it as a present was a vastly different matter from earning it.

"I mean to save up for a motorcycle," Peter declared. "Then I could ride to the tannery every day."

"So you could," agreed Mr. Coddington. "It is not a bad idea. Don't forget, though, that you will be needing clothes now and then. You spoke last night of wanting some flannel shirts to wear to work."

"Yes, but you----"

Mr. Coddington shook his head.

"I have bought your clothes up to this time," he answered, "but now that you have a salary of your own it is time you relieved me of that expense."

"Oh--of--of--course," Peter stammered. "I guess, though, I can get the motorcycle and pay for my clothes, too, without any trouble. How much do clothes cost?"

"Let me see!" Mr. Coddington took out a small expense book and turned its pages rapidly. "Clothing for Peter. Here it is. Last year I spent for you $638."

"For me! For my clothes?" gasped the boy. "Did I spend $638? Why, I had no idea of it! I could have gone without some of those overcoats and things as well as not if I had known they cost so much. That's an awful lot for a boy to spend, isn't it?"

"It's a plenty."

"Why, it's more than I will earn in a whole year."

"Yes, I am afraid it is--at least, for the present."

Peter was thoughtful.

"I can see that it's good-bye to the motorcycle," he said at last, disappointment in every feature.

With an impulsive gesture Mr. Coddington thrust his hand into the breast pocket where his check-book lay; then resolutely took out the hand and put it behind him.

"There seems to be no way but for you to do without a motorcycle for a while, son," he replied. "Do not be discouraged, though. You are now pretty well stocked with the necessary clothing and in consequence will not require many new things for some time. If you are not too proud to wear your old suits to work you can easily put aside some money each week."

"I do not care how old and shabby my clothes are," smiled Peter. "It does not make much difference what I wear to the tannery if I can just have some flannel shirts, overalls, and rubber boots. I've packed away my white tennis suits in moth-balls, you know, since I went into the mill."

They both laughed.

As flannel shirts and overalls were inexpensive and easily obtained, and as Peter already had rubber boots it was possible to begin the saving for the motorcycle without further delay.

In the meantime orders came that Strong was to leave his task of trimming skins and present himself at the beamhouse. Reluctantly he bade farewell to Carmachel and the other men--his first friends at the tannery--and on the following Monday morning he made his way into the long, low room where he had been told the skins were tanned. The room was a revelation, and a none too pleasant one at that! If he had thought the unloading and sorting department unsavory what should he say of this? The floor of the beamhouse was slippery with water, lime, and tanning solutions; unpleasant fumes of wet skins made heavy the air; revolving paddle-wheels suspended from the ceiling dripped upon the passer-by; and men, dragging saturated skins from vats in the floor, piled them in heaps where the water oozing from them trickled out into the general sloppiness and transformed the floor into a great shallow pool of moisture. Back and forth through this wetness moved workmen who, as they wheeled barrows of freshly tanned skins, left a wake of slime behind them. Peter looked about in consternation. The steaming odor of the room was nauseating and filled him with disgust. Could he stand it? And they called this a promotion! What wonder that Carmachel had chuckled when asked what the beamhouse was!

As Peter stood hesitating, a prey to these confused impressions, a lad about his own age touched him on the shoulder.

"Bryant, the foreman, wants to speak to you," he said.

Peter roused himself and followed the boy.

In a corner of the room the foreman greeted him.

"How are you, Strong?" he began. "You see you are no stranger to me, for I have watched you play ball at noon time. I am glad we are to have you in our department."

"Thank you, sir. Yes, Mr. Tyler said I was to report here for the present."

"That's good. We can put you to work, all right. Before you begin, however, I should like to have you look about and get an idea what we do in here. A man always enjoys his work better and does it more intelligently, I contend, if he has some notion of the process in which he is to have a share. Jackson is about your age and has been in this room a long time." (He indicated the boy at Peter's elbow.) "Suppose he takes you around and shows you what happens to the skins after they are sent in here to us."

"Thank you, sir."

Jackson seemed pleased at the task assigned him.

"I'm glad you are coming into the beamhouse to work, Strong," he ventured timidly. "There are not many boys here my age. You won't like it at first, I'm afraid, but you will soon get used to it."

"I don't believe I shall like it at all," was Peter's rueful reply. "It's an awful place, isn't it?"

"Oh, it's not so bad as it seems. You won't mind it--really you won't. Of course the smell is disagreeable and it is wet and sloppy, too; but Bryant, the foreman, is a mighty white fellow and the men, although mostly foreigners, are pleasant enough. I myself was so thankful to get any work that I did not much care what it was."

"Have you been here long?" questioned Peter.

"Ever since I was old enough to go to work--a year this August."

"And you've been in this room all that time!"

"Yes. It takes quite a while to get a promotion here at the tannery. My pay has been raised to nine dollars, though. Maybe I wasn't glad to get the money! You see, I support my mother." Jackson threw back his head proudly.

"You? You support yourself and your mother?" repeated Peter incredulously.

"Sure I do! Why not?"

"But you--why, you are not much older than I am!"

"I'm sixteen. Mother and I get on very well on what I earn, even though it isn't much. Don't you have anybody to take care of?"

"No."

Jackson regarded Peter with astonishment.

"I should think you would be rich as a lord if you have all your money to yourself!" he exclaimed. "What on earth do you find to do with it?"

Once--and the time was not far passed, either--Peter would have laughed at the naive question; now he answered gravely:

"Oh, I am saving some of it."

"That's right. I can't save a cent at present, but some time I hope to get a better salary and then I shall be able to. Now let's go over to the other end of the room and see where they are putting the skins to soak in those big vats of water to get out the salt and dirt. That's the first thing they do after the skins are sent into the beamhouse. You remember how stiff and hard the dry skins were when you unloaded them. Well, they are put into the great revolving wooden drums that you see overhead and are worked about in borax and water until they become soft. They are washed, too. Then after all the skins have been washed and softened they are thrown into lime and are left there until the fibre swells and the hair is loosened. The men you see with rubber gloves on are the limers. If they did not wear gloves they would get their hands burned and raw, for the lime and the chemicals used in the tan often make the hands and arms very sore."

"But I don't see that the skins that are tossed into the lime pits come out with the hair off," objected Peter.

"Bless your heart--the lime does not take the hair off. The men who unhair them have to do that. They lay the wet skins out on boards and with sharp knives pull and scrape off all the white hair."

"Why don't they take off the brown or black hair as well?"

"Because only the white hair is removed by hand. That is kept separate and after being dried is sold to dealers for a good price. The colored hair is taken off by machinery and is sold too, but it is not so valuable."

"I suppose plasterers can use hair like that," speculated Peter.

"Yes, and upholsterers," added Jackson.

Peter smiled.

"Carmachel told me nothing in a tannery was wasted," he said. "I was surprised to find that even the lumps of fat and bits of flesh adhering to the skins, together with the parings that came off when the calfskins were trimmed down to an even thickness, were disposed of for glue stock or fertilizer."

"Every scrap of stuff is used, I can tell you!" assented Jackson. "Calfskin, you know, is never split; it is not heavy enough for that. Besides it is more nearly uniform in weight than a skin like a bull's hide, for instance, which is very much heavier about the head. No, calfskin is fairly even and therefore, while wet, is just put between rollers where a thin, sharp blade shaves from the flesh side any part of it that is thicker than any other. It comes out of equal thickness all over. Do you understand?"

Peter nodded.

"And now have you this beamhouse process straight in your head so we can go on?"

Jackson held up his hand and began to check off the successive steps on his fingers:

"The skins are washed until the dirt and salt are out; they are worked in paddle-wheels, if necessary, until soft; they are limed; unhaired; and bated, or puered. By puering I mean that they are put through a liquid that takes out all the lime; if the lime is not carefully soaked out the skins will be burned and hard and cannot be tanned properly. After the puering the short-hairers remove any remaining hairs; the skins are thoroughly washed again, and at last are ready for tanning."

"How are they tanned?"

"Why, by putting them into paddle-wheels filled with the tanning solution where they revolve as many as seven or eight hours. This solution is then changed for a weaker one, and they revolve again for a couple of hours more. Some skins are tanned in a mixture of chemicals which we buy all prepared; we call those chrome tanned. Others are soaked in a vegetable tan of hemlock, oak, chestnut, palmetto roots, gambier, or quebracho."

"Or what?"

"Quebracho!" Jackson rolled out the long word with a gusto. "Quebracho is a tree something like the lignum-vitæ and grows in South America. The hardened gum comes in barrels and looks like rosin; sometimes, instead of being hard, it is shipped in a liquid state in big tank cars. There is about fifteen per cent. of tannin in quebracho and at the tanneries it can be diluted, of course, to any strength desired. We use it altogether here instead of using other vegetable tans."

"But it says in my geography that every one uses oak or hemlock bark," objected Peter, sceptically.

"Well, the Coddington Company doesn't. Bryant says we tan so much leather here that there would be no way of disposing of the quantities of bark left after the tannin had been extracted from it. Besides bark is scarce and expensive; then, too, it takes a car-load of bark to get even a decent amount of tannin and the freighting adds to the cost. Quebracho can be shipped by water and is therefore more economical, and for the varieties of leather we tan here it answers the purpose as well. It is lots of work to get the tannin out of oak or hemlock bark. The bark has to be ground up and put in a leaching-kettle full of water; after it has boiled the liquid is drained off and the tannin extracted. Using quebracho is a much simpler method. Of course we use oak and hemlock bark, though, in the sole leather tanneries over at Elmwood."

Peter regarded Jackson intently.

"How did you come to know so much about all this business?" he asked at last.

"Oh, I don't know much," was the modest answer. "I just wanted to learn what I could while I had the chance. You can't help being curious when you work so long in one room. Bryant saw I was interested and he's explained all the things

I wanted to find out."

"Then maybe you'll pass on some more of your information," laughed Peter, "and tell me why some of the skins are tanned in quebracho and some in chrome."

"As I told you," repeated Jackson good-naturedly, "quebracho is a vegetable tan and chrome a chemical tan. The effect of each of these processes on the skins is different; so the process used depends on what sort of leather is wanted. At many tanneries chrome is used almost entirely for tanning calfskins because the process is so much quicker; chrome takes but about nine hours while quebracho tanning takes two weeks or thereabouts."

"I see. And after the tanning?"

"The skins are inspected while wet and sorted for stock; they are then stamped with a letter or number so they can be identified; they are fat-liquored, and are dyed."

"What is fat-liquored?"

"Fat-liquored means working the skins about in a mixture of soap and oil until they absorb these softening ingredients and become pliable. All leather, whether chrome or vegetable tanned, has to go through this process. The liquid is put into paddle-wheels just as the tanning mixture is. The dyeing is done in paddle-wheels too, and some kinds of leather have in addition a coat of dye rubbed into them by hand. It gives them a better surface."

"What is your work, Jackson?" asked Peter.

"Oh, I've done about everything there is to do in a beamhouse. Just now I am inspecting and sorting the skins after they are tanned."

"What is Mr. Bryant going to set me at?"

"I don't know. You will have to ask him. But no matter what he gives you to do you must not be discouraged, Strong. You were lucky to get any job at all in the tannery. They have turned away lots of boys your age--they do it every day."

Peter bit his lip to keep from smiling.

"I suppose I ought to consider myself lucky," replied he.

"Well, aren't you? To be young, and well, and to know that if you do your best you have a chance to work up to something better? I think it's great! I intend to work up. Some day I may be a partner in Coddingtons'--who knows! Then I'll dress my mother in silk every day in the week and I'll buy an automobile. I'd like to ride in one of those things just once. Did you ever?"

"Yes," admitted Peter cautiously.

"Honest? Wasn't it bully? Where did you go?"

But Peter was spared the difficult task of replying. Instead, Bryant summoned him, and he was given a wheel-barrow filled with wet skins which were to be carried from the soaking vats to the lime pits. All the rest of the morning back and forth he trudged wheeling load after load. It was stupid, dirty work, and he was glad when the noon whistle blew.

"Let's eat our luncheon together, Strong," said Jackson, "that is--unless you have somebody else you want to lunch with."

Peter assented only too gladly. It was far pleasanter to have a boy his own age to speak to than to eat by himself. Besides he liked Jackson.

But even in the fresh breeze that swept the open field, even while playing ball, even at home after a hot bath and clean clothing, Peter could still scent the odor of the beamhouse. It was days before he became accustomed to it and could feel, with Nat Jackson, that he was a lucky boy to have a "job."

CHAPTER IV

PETER'S MAIDEN SPEECH

Peter had been three weeks in the beamhouse and had in that time proved himself so useful that his pay had been raised from six to six dollars and a half a week. Very proud he was of his financial good fortune. With few demands in the way of clothing he was now able to lay aside quite a little sum toward the motorcycle he so much desired. The days at the tannery passed more quickly. Nat Jackson became his chum and the two lads were almost inseparable; they lunched together, played on the ball team, and often spent their Saturday afternoons in taking long walks or going to Nat's house. Peter, however, took great good care that Nat should not visit him.

The omission of this hospitality was not entirely unnoticed by young Jackson, and the conclusion he drew was that Peter lived humbly--perhaps poorly--in lodgings to which he did not consider it suitable to invite a guest. Nat thought this foolish pride on Peter's part and he meant to tell him so some time when they became better acquainted. It was a mistake, argued Nat, to be over-sensitive about one's poverty. If Peter was saving his money surely that was excuse enough. He had a right to live as he pleased. Furthermore what possible difference could it make in their friendship? Nat himself lived simply but very nicely on the meager salary that he earned. He and his mother rented two tiny bedrooms, a sunny little living-room, and a microscopic kitchen in a part of the town which, to be sure, was cheap and ugly; but Mrs. Jackson, Peter soon found, was one of the rare women who could make a home--a real home--almost anywhere. She often laughingly remarked that if she were to dwell in a snow hovel at the North Pole she believed she should cut a window in the side of it and set a pot of flowers there, and Peter could well imagine her doing it.

She was a short, bright-eyed, motherly little person, with a quick appreciation of a joke, and a wonderful knack at cooking. Incidentally she had a quiet voice and chose soft colors in preference to crude ones. Peter gathered from her manner of speech and from the delicate modeling of her hands that at some time in her life she had occupied a very different position from the one she was now filling. But whatever that past might have been he gained no inkling of it either from her or from her son. Bravely, patiently, happily, she made a home for her boy--such a home that Peter Coddington visited it with the keenest pleasure and came away with a vague wonder what it was that those three wee rooms possessed which was lacking in his own richly furnished mansion.

Perhaps if it had not been for the encouragement of Nat and his mother Peter might not have had the grit to master his work at the beamhouse. A wholesome spur these two friends were to his flagging spirits. There was some subtle quality in Nat's mother that made a fellow want to do his very best--to be as much of a man as he could. And yet she said little to urge either of the lads to their task. It was just that she was so proud and so pleased when they did win any good fortune through their own endeavors. And so Peter forged bravely on, prodded by an unformulated desire to do well not only for the sake of his own parents, but that he might not disappoint the faith that Nat and Nat's mother had in him.

Even Mr. Coddington remarked one evening at dinner (and there was a twinkle in his eye when he said it) that he was highly gratified by the reports he heard of "young Strong."

But as the summer advanced and the days grew hotter Mrs. Coddington watched her boy with anxious care and dropped more than one suggestion that it was time they all were off to the shore. None of her suggestions bore fruit, however, and by and by when she saw that Mr. Coddington had no intention of leaving Milburn she ceased to remonstrate further and Peter settled down to work and to keep as comfortable as he could during the hot weather. What a haven his home, with its green lawns and wide verandas, became, after those long, breathless hours in the tannery! Never before had he half appreciated his surroundings. Most of the houses where the men at the factory lived were huddled closely in that dingy part of the town where Nat Jackson's rooms were, and Peter soon discovered that after supper many of the workmen and their families came and sat in the ball field opposite Factory 1 where there was more air, and where some of the men actually slept when the nights were very hot. It was a blessing--that great open space! Peter wondered what they would have done without it.

He had been raising the query mentally one July morning on his way to work after a close, restless night in his big room on the hill. The day was a sultry one; no air stirred, and it was with a sigh that Peter entered the beamhouse. No sooner was he inside, however, than he at once saw that something was wrong. Knots of men were speaking together in undertones and seemed to be far more eager to talk than to take up their daily tasks. Only Bryant, who moved from one group to another, urging, coaxing, commanding, succeeded in compelling them to attend to what they had to do.

"You fellows can do all the talking you want to at noon," he said. "There will be no builders around to-day, I guess."

"They'll do well to keep away!" muttered an angry Swede, threateningly.

"You go to unhairing skins, Olsen," Bryant commanded, putting his hand firmly but kindly on the broad shoulder of the man. "You can scold your wrath all out this noon. Go on."

Sullenly the man obeyed.

"What is the matter?" Peter managed to whisper to Nat Jackson.

"The men are furious; they are threatening to strike," returned Nat in an undertone.

"To strike!" exclaimed Peter. His thoughts flew to his father. "What has happened?" he questioned insistently.

"Didn't you see last night's paper? Haven't you heard? Mr. Coddington is going to put up another tannery. He's going to build it on the ball field!"

"On the ball field! Our field!"

"So the paper says. Of course the land is his. But it does seem pretty tough!"

Peter moved on, dazed.

To take away the field--the one out-of-door spot for luncheon and exercise! To deprive hundreds of stifled creatures of fresh air and sunlight! It was monstrous! Why hadn't his father mentioned the plan? Of course he did not realize what it would mean to the men or he never would have considered it. What would become of all those tired people who nightly left their bare little dwellings and sought a cool evening breeze in the field? Peter knew Nat and his mother always sat there until bedtime and many of the other workmen brought their wives and children. Once the boy had sat there himself. It was an orderly crowd that he had seen--children tumbling over each other on the grass; women seated on the benches and exchanging a bit of gossip; tired men stretched full-length on the turf resting in the quiet of the place.

Why, it was a crime to take the field away!

All the morning while he worked Peter's mind seethed with arguments against the building of the new factory. He longed to see his father and talk it out. Surely Mr. Coddington would listen if he realized the conditions. He was a kind man--not an inhuman brute. It seemed as if the noon whistle would never blow.

With Nat Jackson and a score of agitated workmen Peter went out into the shade opposite. Luncheon was forgotten, and ball, too. Instead a crowd gathered and on every hand there were mutterings and angry protests.

"Of course Coddington can take the land. It's his. There is no law to prevent him from doing anything he wants to with it. What does he care for us?" remarked an old, gray-haired tanner.

"The working man is nothing to the rich man," grumbled another. "All the millionaire wants is more money. Another factory means just that--more money! It's money, money, money--always money with the rich. The more they have the more they want."

Sick at heart, Peter listened.

"Why don't you fellows do something about it?" blustered a red-faced Italian. "I'll bet you if we called a strike it would bring Coddington to terms. He'd a good sight rather give up building that factory than have us all walk out-- 'specially now when there's more work ahead than the firm can handle. I've been in five strikes in other places and we never failed yet to get what we started for."

"Do you think you could drive a man like Mr. Coddington that way?" It was Carmachel who spoke. "You can walk out, all of you, if you choose. It would make no difference to him. If he has decided it is best to put up that tannery he'll put it up. A strike would do you no good and as a result your families would be without food and a roof over their heads all winter. You're a fine man, Ristori! Coddington pays you well. You take his money and are glad to get a job from him; then the first minute anything does not go to suit you you turn against him and cry: Strike! You don't know what loyalty means. Hasn't Coddington always been square with you? Hasn't he paid you good wages? Hasn't he added an extra bit to your envelope at Christmas? I'll not strike!"

"What would you have us do?" was Ristori's hot retort. "Would you have us sit by like dumb things and let him do anything to us he pleases?"

"Coddington is a reasonable man," Carmachel replied. "Why don't some of you talk decently with him about all this?"

"Aye! And lose our jobs for our pains!" sneered a swarthy Armenian.

A shout went up.

"A strike! A strike!" yelled a hundred voices.

"Would you strike and see your families starve?" cried Nat Jackson. "I have a mother to support. I care more for her than for the field and everything on it. I shall not strike."

"You white-livered young idiot!" roared some one in the crowd.

"I tell you, men," went on Carmachel, "there is nothing to be gained by striking. Get together some of your best speakers from each factory and let them ask an interview of Mr. Coddington--now--this afternoon--before anything more is done about the new factory."

"He'll not grant it!"

"Hasn't he always been fair with you?"

"Yes!"

"Aye!"

"So he has!"

"He has that!"

Grudgingly the workmen admitted it, even the most rabid of them.

Drawn by an irresistible impulse Peter elbowed his way into the midst of the workmen.

"I am sure Mr. Coddington will listen to you," he ejaculated earnestly. "Choose your men and let them go to him. Give him a chance to see your side of it. He will be reasonable--I know he will."

"It's the Little Giant," said one man to another.

"Put it to vote," urged Peter. "Come! How many are for going to Mr. Coddington? You fellows do not want a strike. Think what it would mean!"

"The lad's right. Up with the hands!"

It was a crisis.

Peter trembled from head to foot.

A few hands were raised, then slowly a few more; more came. All over the field they shot into the air.

"And now choose your representatives," called Peter quickly, dreading lest the tide of sentiment should turn.

"Carmachel! He doesn't seem to fear losing his job," piped a voice. "Put on Carmachel!"

"And Jackson; he said he would not strike anyway," called somebody else.

"Bryant is a good fellow! Put Bryant on."

"Put on some men from the other factories, too," demanded a Pole aggressively.

A committee of twelve were chosen.

"Add the Little Giant as the thirteenth--just for luck!" laughed a knee-staker.

There was a cry of approval.

"The Little Giant! The Little Giant!" rose in a chorus.

"No! No, indeed! I couldn't!" Peter protested violently.

"Of course you could!" contradicted Carmachel. "Come, come! You mustn't be so modest, Strong. You are with us for keeping the field, aren't you?"

"Yes. But there are reasons that you don't understand why I couldn't----"

"Pooh! What reasons?"

"I can't tell you. But I couldn't possibly go to Mr. Coddington with the men--I couldn't, really, Carmachel," reiterated Peter miserably.

"Nonsense! The only question is this--is your sympathy with us or isn't it?"

"Of course it is!" There was no doubting the fervor of the avowal.

"Then that settles it. Although you have come here but recently, Strong, we all consider you a friend and count you as one of ourselves. You'll stand by the bunch, won't you?" Carmachel scrutinized Peter sharply.

"Yes, I will. But you don't understand the circumstances or you would never urge me to----"

Carmachel interrupted him.

"I guess I understand the circumstances better than you think," returned he, dryly. "Mr. Coddington got you your place, I've heard. Naturally you feel under obligations to him for his kindness. That's all very well. But has he ever been near you since he put you into the tannery? No! He sits in his office and opens his mail and you are just a boy in the works. Isn't that so? What's to hinder you from going respectfully to him with the rest of us and calling to his attention something which seems to us an injustice? You said yourself it was the best plan. You pleaded with us to do it."

"I know."

"Then why won't you go yourself? You're not a coward, Strong, nor, unless I greatly mistake, are you the sort of chap who would point out to others a path he wouldn't dare follow himself."

"I'll go!" cried Peter suddenly. "I'll go, but I will not do any speaking."

"Nobody wants you to speak," growled an Italian who had been standing near and who had overheard the conversation. "Bryant, Carmachel, and the older men will do the speaking. It's their place."

So it was agreed.

Events shaped themselves rapidly. Within an hour Mr. Coddington, seated in his perfectly appointed office, received word that a deputation of his men respectfully requested an interview with him that afternoon.

He was thunderstruck.

What did the demand foreshadow? Was a strike brewing? The men had appeared perfectly satisfied with the working conditions at the tanneries. Wages were fairly high and the factories conformed to every requirement of the Health and Labor Laws.

He touched a bell.

"Ask Tyler to step here," said he, frowning.

Mr. Tyler entered hastily.

"What's all this, Tyler?" demanded his chief. "I hear the men want to see me."

"I know nothing about it, sir. They've kept their own council. If they have a grievance they have not told me."

"No labor agitators have been in town recently?"

"Not to my knowledge, Mr. Coddington."

"That will do."

Tyler went out.

Again Mr. Coddington rang.

"I will see the men at three o'clock," he said to a messenger.

Left alone the president paced the floor. Business was good. The books showed a quantity of unfilled orders. It would be an awkward time for a strike.

"Undoubtedly I could get strike-breakers from Chicago," he murmured aloud, "but it would take time. Besides, I do not want my men to walk out. Think of the years many of them have worked here! The town will be full of idle persons and suffering families. I have never had a strike in all the history of my business. I've always tried to do what was fair toward those who were in my employ. That is what cuts--to be square with your men and then have them meet you with ingratitude. Why, I would have staked my oath that they would have stood by me. I'm disappointed--disappointed!"

With such unpleasant reflections as companions three o'clock came none too speedily for Mr. Coddington. The men were ushered promptly into the office and the door closed. Then an awkward silence ensued. Nobody knew exactly whose place it was to speak first.

But if the tanners had expected the president of the company to break the ice and open the interview they had missed their calculations, for he did no such thing. He met their gaze firmly, courteously, but silently.

Peter, who stood at the back of the room behind the older workmen, saw in his father's face an unaccustomed sternness and felt instinctively that their mission was destined to failure.

It was Bryant who at last summoned courage to begin the conference.

"Mr. Coddington," he said, "we men have come to you because we wish to hear the truth concerning a rumor that has reached us. We come respectfully. You are our chief--the one who, in the past, has always been fair and square with us. It is because of your justice that we address you now. Is it true that you propose to take the vacant field opposite Factory 1 for the site of a new building?"

As Mr. Coddington drew a sigh of relief he inclined his head.

"You have been correctly informed," he assented. "We need more room. The land is lying idle with a tax to be paid yearly upon it. It seems to me an economic plan to utilize the space for a new factory in which the patent leather department may be housed."

"Did you realize, in deciding, that the field you intend to take is the recreation ground of the men in your mills?" asked Bryant.

"I know that some of the men play ball there," replied Mr. Coddington, smiling.

"And yet you have decided to take it in spite of that fact?"

The president stiffened.

"The land," said he, "is mine, and the taxes I annually pay on it render it rather a costly spot for a ball field. For years the lot has been nothing but an expense to me. If the case were yours and you could derive an income from property where previously all had been outgo wouldn't you do it?"

"But do you need that income, Mr. Coddington?" cut in one of the men. "Isn't the Coddington Company rich? Must rich men go on getting more and more, and never think of those who coin their money for them?"

It was an unwise speech, and its effect was electrical.

"I will try and believe that you men came here with the intention of being courteous," observed Mr. Coddington with frigid politeness. "My affairs, however, are mine and not yours. I must deal with them in the way that I consider wisest. You hardly realize, I think, that you are over-stepping the bounds of propriety when you attempt to dictate to me what I shall do with my land, or how I shall manage my tanneries."

The sternness of the answer blocked any possible reply.

Amid the silence of the room one could almost hear the heart-beats of the waiting throng.

Then some one in the crowd made his way to the front of the room and faced the president.

It was Peter Strong.

As Mr. Coddington's gaze fell on his son he started.

The boy stood erect and looked his father squarely in the eye.

"May I speak, sir?"

Mr. Coddington bowed.

Peter began gently, respectfully, and his words were without defiance.

[Illustration: "MAY I SPEAK, SIR?"]

"I hardly think you know what the field you are going to take from the men-- from us all--means, sir. Not only do we play ball and go there to eat our luncheon but each noon time we have a chance to get a breath of fresh air and go back to work better in consequence. The field, moreover, is the only open lot in this part of the town. At night hundreds of men who have worked hard all day congregate there to get sight of the green grass and enjoy a little interval of quiet. They bring their families from the huddled districts where there is neither sky, tree, nor breathing space. Suppose you lived as they do? Suppose when you went home at night it was to a tenement in a crowded part of the city? You return to a big house on the top of a hill where the trees catch every breeze that passes; where there are shrubs, gardens, flowers. Who needs this space more-- you or your employees?"

When he began to speak, Peter had had no clear idea of what he should say; but as he went on words came to him. Was not he himself one of these working men who knew what the heat, the odor, the noise of the tanneries meant? As he went on his voice vibrated with earnestness. There was no doubting his sincerity. It was in truth Peter Strong and not Peter Coddington who made the appeal.

As Mr. Coddington listened without comment to the speech his wordlessness was an enigma to the men. It seemed as if it was a silence of suppressed anger and in consternation Carmachel plucked Peter's sleeve.

"Say no more, lad," he whispered. "You've gone too far. You forget that it is the president himself you're talking to. You shouldn't have said what you did, even though it's true."

But Peter scarcely heard.

He was watching his father--watching his face for the gleam that did not come.

"I will consider what you have said, Strong," replied Mr. Coddington after a pause. "I will acknowledge that I was ignorant of the fact that the spot meant anything to the people of the community. If the conditions are as you say we may be able to find a solution for the problem. May we consider this interview at an end?"

Although the remark was in the form of a question the committee felt itself dismissed and uncomfortably the men filed into the corridor.

"We've gained nothing!" was Bryant's first word when they found themselves alone. "We've only succeeded in antagonizing Mr. Coddington and solidified his intention of taking the field. We might have got somewhere if Strong had not put his foot in it. What possessed you to pitch into the president like that, young fellow?"

"What made you speak at all?" put in Carmachel. "Don't you know your place better than to think a rich man like Mr. Coddington is going to stand for having a kid like you lay down the law to him? How ever did you dare? Your job is gone--that's certain. I'm sorry, too, for we all like you here at the works."

"Oh, Peter! Peter! Why did you say it?" wailed Nat Jackson. "I know you had the best of intentions, but don't you see that you've upset the whole thing?"

There was something very like a sob in Nat's tone.

Poor Peter! From every hand came reproaches. If only he had not spoken! His impulse, good at heart, had been one of mistaken zeal. It was not that he himself had lost his cause--he had lost it for hundreds of men in whom he had become interested, and whom he had struggled to serve.

Very wretched the boy was for the remainder of the day; when night came he dreaded to go home. What would his father say to him?

Peter might have saved himself this worry, for when he entered the dining-room and sat down to dinner he found the good-humor of his father quite undisturbed and no allusion was made to the day's occurrence. Surely this was carrying out to the letter the agreement they had made. Peter Coddington was his son and he treated him as such; but to Peter Strong, the boy of the tannery, he had nothing to say. Miserably Peter waited for the opportunity to offer explanation or apology. It did not come and all chance for securing it vanished when, directly after the coffee was served, Mr. Coddington rose, announced that he had an engagement, and was whirled off in the motor-car. He did not return until long after his son was asleep.

Had Peter known what this mysterious engagement was his slumbers would have been happier, for the president of the company had gone on no idle errand. Screened from view in the far corner of the big touring-car he had ridden past the tanneries and with his own eyes had seen the benches in the ball field thronged with sweltering humanity. Twice, three times he passed. He saw the boys at their games; the tired mothers resting in the twilight; the babies that toddled at their feet; and the men--his men--lying full-length on the grass drinking in the cool air. This was what he had come out to see.

The result of it was that the next morning, in the doorway of every factory of the Coddington Company, the following notice was posted:

After careful investigation Mr. Coddington has decided that it is for the interest of his men that the plan to erect a building on the ball field be abandoned. Instead the land will be laid out as a recreation ground to be known as Strong Park, and to be reserved for the Coddington employees, their families, and their friends. Negotiations have been opened for a site on Central Street, where the new patent leather factory will shortly be erected.

Signed: H. M. CODDINGTON, President.

What an ovation the men gave Peter that day! And how grateful Peter was to his father! So grateful that before going to bed he felt compelled to break their compact of silence and exclaim:

"Father, it's splendid of you to keep the field for the men! I can't thank you half enough, sir. But you ought not to name it after me."

"I'm not naming it after you," was his father's laconic reply. "I'm naming it after Peter Strong."

CHAPTER V

A CATASTROPHE

In an incredibly short space of time Strong Park began to be a reality. Men commenced grading its uneven turf; laying out walks and flower-beds; erecting benches and a band stand, and setting out trees and shrubs. An ample area at one end of the grounds was reserved for a ball field; and adjoining it parallel bars, traveling rings, and the apparatus necessary to an out-of-door gymnasium was put in place.

All these arrangements Peter witnessed with delight. He longed to tell his father so, but unfortunately was granted no opportunity. Once, and once only, did Mr. Coddington refer to the project and that was to inquire whimsically of Peter if his friend Strong was satisfied with the preparations, and whether he had any suggestions to make. Young Strong had no suggestions, Peter declared. He thought the park perfect. And indeed it was! Neither thought nor money had been spared to make it so.

Peter was very proud of his father those days when, on every hand, he heard the men extolling the president's generosity. More than once the great secret of his relation to the Coddingtons trembled on his lips and almost slipped from him, but he succeeded in holding it resolutely in check. Despite his intimacy with Nat and his frequent visits to the Jackson home not a hint of his real identity escaped him. His assumed rôle was made easier, perhaps, by the fact that he had entered so heartily into it. He was really living the career of Peter Strong, and the Peter Coddington who had idled away so many months in purposeless, irresponsible dallying was rapidly becoming but a hazy memory. There was no denying that Peter Strong's life was the far more interesting one--every day it became more absorbing.

"You see we're really doing something!" exclaimed Peter enthusiastically to Nat Jackson one Saturday afternoon when they were taking one of their long tramps together. "Washing and carting skins isn't much in itself, and it would not be any fun at all if it wasn't part of the chain. But when you think how necessary a step in the process it is, and consider that there could be no leather unless somebody did just what I am doing, it seems well worth while. I never did anything before that was actually necessary. It is rather good sport."

And, in truth, Peter was doing something. Had he doubted it the ever increasing fund toward his motorcycle would have been a tangible proof. Already it was quite a little nest-egg and the boy, who had never before earned a penny, felt justifiably proud of the crisp bills that he was able to tuck at intervals into the bank. Once more, as a recognition of his faithful work, his pay had been raised--this time to seven dollars.

It was toward the middle of August that Mr. Tyler, the superintendent, who evidently was keeping closer watch of Peter's progress than he had suspected, notified him that on the fifteenth he was to leave the beamhouse and report in the finishing department. Peter was not only astonished but a good deal distressed. He had worked not a whit harder or more faithfully than had Nat Jackson, and deserved the promotion no more--in fact not as much as his chum. It seemed grossly unfair. Peter turned the matter over and over in his mind. He would have rejoiced in the good fortune had he considered it came to him justly; but to take what belonged to somebody else--that robbed it of all its charm. He thought and thought what he should do and at last he gained courage to go to Mr. Tyler with his dilemma. An appeal for his friend could do no harm and it might do good.

When he had made his errand known the superintendent tilted back in his chair and regarded him in silence.

"Jackson is far better informed as to the processes than I am, Mr. Tyler," Peter pleaded. "Besides, he has a mother to support and needs to get on. If there is only one vacancy in the finishing department can't you give him the chance? He has been a year in the beamhouse already, and if there is a promotion it belongs by right to him."

Mr. Tyler fingered his watch-chain. He had never had precisely this experience before--to try to push a man and have him beg that you give his good luck to somebody else. Surely this Peter Strong was an extraordinary person! Mr. Tyler could now understand how even the president of the company, under the spell of his simple eloquence, had not only surrendered a valuable building lot for a park but had actually named it after the youthful enthusiast. The superintendent couldn't but admire the lad's earnestness. At the same time, however, he did not at all fancy having his plans questioned or interfered with; therefore when he spoke it was to dash Peter's demands to earth with a rebuff.

"Most men would hail with gratitude an opening that took them out of the beamhouse, Strong," replied he stiffly. "It is generous of you, no doubt, to make this plea for your friend, but you see you are the person recommended for the promotion. In this world we must take our chances as they come. Unfortunately the opportunities of life are not transferable, my boy. I will, however, bear Jackson in mind and see if anything can be done for him. Good-morning."

The nod of Mr. Tyler's head was final.

Peter turned away, heart-sick at his failure. He had done all he could unless, indeed, he broke his bond and appealed to his father, and any such breach of their contract he considered out of the question. Yet how he dreaded to tell the Jacksons of his success. Nat would be so hurt! Still, they must, of course, know it in time and how much better to hear the news from Peter himself than in cowardly fashion to leave the spread of the tidings to rumor. Accordingly he told his tale as bravely as he could.

"It isn't as if I deserved it one bit more than you, Nat," he concluded. "It has just happened to come to me--I've no idea why."

"Of course you deserve it, Peter," cried Nat. "Haven't you worked like a tiger in the beamhouse ever since you came here? You know you have. Everybody says so. There isn't a man in the works but likes you and will be glad at your good luck--I most of all. Some day I'll be making a start up the ladder myself; wait and see if I don't!"

Although he spoke with a generous heartiness and made every attempt to conceal his chagrin, Peter knew that in reality Nat honestly felt that he had failed to receive the prize that he had rightfully won. Had not the friendship of the boys been of tough fibre it would have been shattered then and there. As it was their affection for each other bridged the chasm and it would have been hard to tell which of them suffered the more--the lad who through no fault of his own had taken the award that belonged to his chum, or the lad who had won the prize only to see it handed to some one else. Peter, who was the victim of success, seemed of the two the more overwhelmed with regrets and therefore it was Nat who, despite his bitter disappointment, turned comforter.

"You mustn't be so cut up over it, Peter, old boy! Of course I know you didn't have anything to do with it. The men in a factory are like so many checkers-- they are moved about just any way that those higher up choose to play the game. It is all right and I want you to know I think so. Don't start in at your new job feeling that I'm sorry you have it. I'm glad; really I am, Peter!"

"It's mighty decent of you, Nat. I wish I had the chance to show you how much I appreciate it."

"I don't want you to show me; I just want you to believe that I mean what I say. And you mustn't mind our working in different departments. We'll be together at noon time just the same. It won't make any difference."

But still Peter was not happy. Day after day he waited hopefully to see if Mr. Tyler would make good his promise and do something for young Jackson; but nothing came of it, and no course remained but to accept unwillingly the promotion and set his foot on this upward rung of the ladder.

The finishing department occupied several floors of the building devoted to calfskins, and the first task given Peter was to help stretch and tack the skins which were still wet from dyeing on boards, after which they were dried by steam in a large, hot room. In some factories, he learned, the skins were put in great rooms with open shutters on all sides, where they dried in the air. But the Coddington Company, he was told, preferred drying by steam. Peter was very slow at tacking the wet skins on the boards. The speed with which the boys worked who had been long at the job astounded him. With lightning swiftness they took up the big, flat-headed tacks, placed, and struck them. One could scarcely follow the motions of their hands. Fortunately for Peter he was released from this work after a few days and set to helping the men who measured the finished skins in an automatic measuring machine; this machine recorded the dimensions of the skins on a dial and was a wonderfully intricate contrivance. Try as he would Peter was unable to fathom how it could so quickly and exactly compute a problem that it would have taken him a long time to solve.

Incidentally he learned many other things of the workmen. Some of the very stiff calfskins, he discovered, were "dusted" or laid in bins of damp sawdust and softened before they were taken to the finishers. There were a multitude of processes, he found, for converting the leather into the special kinds desired. What a numberless variety of finishes there was! There was willow calf--a fine, soft, chrome-tanned leather which, the foreman told him, was put into the best quality of men's and women's shoes; box calf--a high grade, storm-proof leather, chrome tanned and dull finished; chrome calf--finished in tan color, and with a fine, smooth grain; boarded calf--tanned either in chrome or quebracho; wax calf--finished by polishing the flesh side until it took a hard, waxy surface; mat calf that was dull in finish; storm calf, oiled for winter wear; and French calf, which, like wax calf, was finished on the flesh side.

"How in the world could any one think of so many different things to do to the skin of a calf?" ejaculated Peter.

His head fairly ached with the information poured into it by the zealous foreman who, by the way, was an Englishman named Stuart.

"In time you'll sort out all I have told you," Stuart answered encouragingly, observing Peter's despair. "It is simple enough when you once understand the different finishing processes. First the leather is rolled by machinery until it is pliable enough for the finishers to work on. Then it goes through a 'putting out' process; by that I mean that it is laid out on benches where it is stretched and flattened by being smoothed with a piece of hard rubber; next the edges are trimmed off and the odd bits sold; some of these go to hardware dealers who use them for washers or for the thousand and one purposes that leather is needed for in making tools."

"More economy!" put in Peter.

"Yes, I guess you have learned already that we do not waste much here," grinned Stuart.

Peter nodded.

"Afterward," Stuart continued, "follow the many methods for getting certain varieties of finish on the leather. Here, for instance, you will see men graining tan stock by working it by hand into tiny wrinkles; they use heavy pieces of cork with which they knead the material until the leather is checked in minute squares. It looks like an easy thing to do, but it isn't. It requires skilled workmen in order to get satisfactory results. Over here," and he beckoned to Peter, "men are making 'boarded calf' by beating and pounding it as you see, that they may get fine, soft stock. Here still others are glassing the leather and giving it a smooth surface by rubbing it with a heavy piece of glass."

"And what are those fellows over by the wall doing?" inquired Peter, pointing to a group of workmen who, with right leg naked, were standing in a row and rapidly drawing tan leather first over a wooden upright set in the floor, and then over their knee.

"Those," Stuart answered, "are knee-stakers. Strangely enough no machine has yet been invented which will give to certain kinds of leather the elasticity and softness which can be put into it by a man's stretching it over his bare knee. It is a curious way to earn one's living, isn't it? See how quickly they work and how strong they are. Just look how the muscles of their legs stand out!"

"I should say so," Peter answered. "Why, it almost seems as if they must have been track sprinters all their lives. They must be well paid."

"What they earn depends on how fast they work," Stuart said. "All this finishing is piece work. The more a man can do in an hour the higher he is paid. Almost all these fellows are skilled workmen who have been at just this task for a long time. They do it rapidly and well, and receive good wages."

Stuart walked on and Peter followed.

"Here is a machine that makes gun-metal finished leather for the uppers of black shoes; the leather is, as you see, put through a series of rollers where it is blacked, oiled, and ironed, and comes out with that dull surface."

"Are all these different kinds of leather really made from calfskins?" asked Peter at last.

"Practically so--yes," replied Stuart. "Upper or dressed leather is made from large calfskins or else from kips. Kips, you know, are the skins of under-sized cows, oxen, horses, buffalo, walrus, and other such animals. These are tanned and sorted out in the beamhouse when wet. The thick ones are usually split thin by machinery and the two parts are finished separately. The part of the leather where the hair grew is the more valuable and is called the grain; the other part which was next to the animal is called the split. Remember those two terms-- the grain and the split."

"I'll try my best," said Peter with a doubtful shake of his head. "I am dreadfully afraid, though, that I shall forget some of the things you have told me to-day."

"I don't expect you to remember all I've told you, Strong," laughed Stuart, good-naturedly. "Why, you would not be a human, breathing boy if you did. It has taken me a long time to learn the facts that I have been telling you. But do remember about the grain and the split; and while you are remembering that, try also to remember that a rough split is the cheapest leather made. Some heavy hides are split two, four, and even six times and are then sold. You can see this sort of leather up-stairs in the shipping-room of the other factory, and if I were you I would take the trouble to go up there some time and look at it. You may be interested, too, to know----"

But what the interesting item was Peter never found out.

A boy, breathless from running, came rushing into the room.

"If you please, sir," he panted, "Mr. Bryant sent me to find Peter Strong! Young Jackson has been hurt. He slipped on the wet floor and the wheel of a heavy truck went over his ankle. Jackson says it is only a sprain, but Mr. Bryant thinks the bones are broken. They've telephoned for a doctor. Jackson is lying on the floor awful white and still, and he says he wants Peter Strong. Mr. Bryant told me to tell you to send him right away."

Peter needed no second bidding. Down the stairs he flew.

Only yesterday he had longed for a chance to prove his friendship for Nat.

Now, all unsolicited, the opportunity had come.

CHAPTER VI

TWO PETERS AND WHICH WON

Aflutter with anxiety, Peter followed the messenger back to the beamhouse.

Of all people why should this calamity come to Jackson? In addition to the suffering that must of necessity accompany such a disaster Peter reflected, as he went along, that Nat could ill afford to lose his wages and incur the expense of doctor's bills. Poor Nat! It seemed as if he had none of the good luck he deserved--only disappointment and misfortune.

Peter found his chum stretched on the floor in a dark little entry adjoining the workroom, with Bryant keeping guard.

"I am down and out this time, no mistake, Pete!" called Nat with a rather dubious attempt to be cheerful. "You see what happens when you go off into another department and leave me. I was all right while you were here."

Peter knelt beside him.

"I'm mighty sorry, old chap," he said. "Does it hurt much?"

As Jackson tried to turn, his lips whitened with pain.

"Well, rather! I guess, though, I'll be all right in a few days. It's only a sprain."

As Peter glanced questioningly at Bryant, who was standing in the shadow, the older man shook his head and put his finger to his lips.

"Well, anyway, Nat," answered Peter, trying to feign a gaiety he did not feel, "you will at least get a vacation. I told you only the other day you needed one."

"I don't need it any more than you do, Peter. Besides I can't stop work, no matter what happens. What would become of my mother, and who would pay our rent if my money stopped coming in? No sir-e-e! I shall get this foot bandaged up and be back at the tannery to-morrow. The doctor can fix it so I can keep at work, can't he, Mr. Bryant?"

"I hope so, Jackson," replied Bryant, kindly. "We'll see when he comes."

But the doctor was far less optimistic. He examined the ankle, pronounced it fractured, and ordered Nat to the hospital where an X-ray could be taken before the bones were set.

Nat, who had endured the pain like a Spartan, burst into tears.

"What will become of us--of my mother, Peter?" he moaned.

"Now don't you get all fussed up, Nat," said Peter soothingly. "Leave things to me. I'll take care of your mother and attend to the house rent. I have plenty of money. You know I have been saving it up ever since I came here."

"Oh, but Peter--I couldn't think of taking your money!" Nat protested.

"Stuff! Of course you can take it! I should like to know whose money you would take if not mine. Anyway you can't help yourself. I have you in my power now and you've got to do just as I say."

"But I don't see how I can ever pay it back, Peter."

"No matter."

"It does matter."

"Well, well! We will settle all that later. Don't worry about it. I am only too thankful that I have the money to help you out," was Peter's earnest response. "I'd be a great kind of a chum if I didn't stick by you when you are in a hole like this. You'd do the same for me."

"You bet I would!"

"Of course! Well, what's the difference?"

"I'm afraid I'll have to take you at your word, Peter," agreed Nat reluctantly, after an interval of reflection. "I do not just see what else I can do at present."

"That's the way to talk," cried Peter triumphantly. "I'll look out for everything. See! They have come with a motor-car to take you to the hospital! You are going to have your long-coveted ride in an automobile, Nat."

Nat laughed in spite of himself.

"I'm not so keen about it as I was."

Gently the men lifted him in and the doctor followed.

"I'll be out in a week, Peter--sure thing!" called Nat shutting his lips tightly together to stifle a moan as the car shot ahead.

"A week, indeed!" sniffed Bryant, as he turned away. "It'll be nearer a month. So Jackson has a mother to look after, has he?"

"Yes, sir."

"Well, suppose you go right over there and ease her mind about this accident before she hears of it through somebody else. Tell her there is no cause for alarm. The boy will have the best of care at the hospital, and she can go there and see him every day during visiting hours."

"And you think it will be a month before he will be about again, Mr. Bryant?" questioned Peter, anxiously.

"Oh, I'm no doctor. How can I tell?" was Bryant's somewhat testy answer. "One thing is certain, however; he won't be here again this week. Sprint along."

And so it was Peter Strong who bore the sorry tidings to Nat's mother, and who cheered and encouraged her as affectionately as if he had been her own son; it was also Peter who, during the weeks that followed, paid the Jacksons' rent and provided sufficient funds for living expenses. How he blessed his motorcycle savings! Without them he never could have helped Nat at this time when help was so sorely needed. Far from begrudging the money Peter exulted in spending it. A motorcycle seemed singularly unimportant when contrasted with a crisis like this. Yet magnificent as his little fortune had seemed it dwindled rapidly. How much everything cost! How had Nat ever managed to keep soul and body together on what he earned? Peter's savings melted like the snows before the warm spring sunshine, and one day the lad awoke to the fact that there was no more money in the bank and that Nat's mother was absolutely dependent for food upon his daily earnings. It was a new sensation and a startling one--to know that you must work--that if you stopped some one dear to you would go hungry.

Poor Peter!

He now had a spur indeed--an incentive to toil as he never had toiled before!

Stuart was delighted with his recently acquired pupil.

"He is as steady a little chap as you would care to see," he told Bryant when they met in the yard one day. "And he is bright as a button, too. Already he has caught on to the various finishing processes and is as handy as any of the men in the department. And then he is such a well spoken lad; not like many of the boys who come into the tannery. He must have come of good family. Do you know anything about his people?"

"Not a thing. I've heard that Mr. Coddington got him his job in the first place, but that may not be true; I think, though, it is more than likely, because they have pushed him ahead faster than is customary. But at any rate the boy has made good, no matter who started him. He will be at the top of the ladder yet."

Peter Strong, however, was not thinking at the present time of the top of the ladder. His mind was entirely set upon relieving the worry of his sick chum and providing the necessary comforts for Mrs. Jackson. Only on Saturdays had he time to go to the hospital and see Nat; but he wrote long letters--jolly, cheery letters, which he dashed off every night before going to bed.

"About every man in the tannery has inquired for you, Nat," he wrote, "and pretty soon I am going to charge a fee for information. Your mother is all right, and declares that she now has two sons instead of one. You better hurry up and come home, or she may decide she likes me better than she does you!"

How Nat laughed when he read that message! The very idea!

Of all this busy life and its varied interests Peter's family knew nothing. His father and mother had gone for a month's trip to the Catskills and there was no one but the servants at home to tell his troubles to had he wished to unburden his worries. So he plodded bravely on alone. How glad he was that the beamhouse was left behind, and that during those warm September days he could work in a large, well-ventilated room where there was fresher air. Perhaps, however, he grew a little thin under his unaccustomed load of anxiety, for when his father and mother returned from their vacation Peter was conscious more than once of his father's fixed gaze, and one evening when the boy was going to bed there was a knock at the door and Mr. Coddington entered the room. For a few seconds he roamed uneasily about, straightening a picture here and an ornament there; then he said abruptly:

"Well, Peter--the summer is almost over. Here it is nearly the middle of

September! I fancy the weeks have gone pretty slowly with your friend Strong. What do you say to quitting the tannery and going back to school?"

Peter's breath almost stopped. He had not dreamed of leaving his work. Such a myriad of thoughts arose at the bare suggestion that he could not answer.

Mr. Coddington misunderstood his silence.

"Of course you are astonished, my boy, and not a little glad, I imagine. When I sent you to the tannery, however, I did not intend to keep you there permanently. I simply wanted to wake you up to doing something and make you prove the stuff you were made of. You have done that and more too. I have heard nothing but the best reports, and I am proud of you, Peter. The tannery has served its purpose for the present. Suppose we leave it now for a while."

Still Peter did not speak.

"Perhaps you are disappointed to stop short of earning money enough for your motorcycle," suggested Mr. Coddington, puzzled by the lad's silence. "Is that it? Tell me now, how much would you need to put with what you have already saved? Do you recall the sum you have in the bank?"

"I haven't any money in the bank, Father," was Peter's unwilling reply.

"What! Not a cent?"

Peter shook his head.

"Have you drawn it out and spent it all?"

"Yes, sir."

"I'm sorry to hear that--sorry, and a little disappointed. However, we mustn't expect too much of you. Come now, what do you say to my proposition of returning to school?"

"I can't do it, sir."

"What!"

"I'm afraid you can't quite understand, sir. You see Peter Coddington would like to go back, but Peter Strong won't let him. Peter Strong must stay at the tannery, Father. He can't leave. There are reasons why it isn't possible," Peter blurted out incoherently.

"What reasons?" demanded his father. "You've not been getting into trouble, Peter?"

"No, sir."

Mr. Coddington looked baffled--baffled, and displeased.

Poor Peter! He longed to explain, but a strange reticence held him back. He had never mentioned at home either Strong's affairs or his friends and it now seemed well-nigh impossible to make any one--even his own father-- understand how much he cared for Nat, and what this disaster had meant to them both; besides, it was too much like blowing his own trumpet to sit up and tell his father how he had played fairy godmother to the Jacksons. It would sound as if he wanted praise, and Peter, who was naturally a modest lad, shrank from anything of the sort. Accordingly he said never a word.

Mr. Coddington wandered to the window and drummed nervously on the pane.

"You have no more explanations to make to me, Peter?" he asked at last, turning and facing his son.

"I--I'm afraid not, sir. You see it is hard to explain things. No one would understand," faltered the boy.

Chagrined as he was, Mr. Coddington strove to be patient.

"Come now, Peter," he urged, "no matter what you've done let's out with it. Maybe I've made a mistake in not allowing you to talk more freely here at home about your affairs at the tannery. It certainly seems to have resulted in making you less frank with me than you used to be. Let us put all that behind us now. Just what sort of trouble have you got into down there?"

Words trembled on Peter's lips. Would it be loyal to tell his father--to tell any one, all the Jacksons' affairs? Nat had told them in confidence and had not expected they would be passed on to anybody else. No, he must keep that trust sacred. He must tell no one.

"I can't tell you, Father," he said. "I'll come out all right, though. Don't worry about me. I've just got to keep on working at the tannery as hard as I can."

"Are you trying to pay up something?" inquired his father, an inspiration seizing him.

"Yes, sir."

Mr. Coddington realized that further attempts to get at the truth were useless, and not a little perturbed he left the room.

All the next day Peter was haunted by reproaches. It took no very keen vision to detect that his father was worried, and this worry the boy felt he must relieve. His course lay clearly outlined before him; he would go to the hospital and ask Nat's permission to tell the entire story. Much as Peter disliked to speak of what he had done to help the Jacksons it was far preferable to having his father suffer the present anxiety.

Accordingly when Saturday afternoon came Peter set forth to make his appeal to Nat. It was not until he almost reached the hospital that a new and disconcerting thought complicated the action which but a few moments before had appeared so simple. How was he to explain to Nat this intimacy with Mr. Coddington? The president of the company, Nat knew as well as he, had not been near Peter since he entered the tannery. Why should young Strong suddenly be venturing to approach this august personage with his petty troubles? Of course Nat wouldn't understand--no, nor anybody else for that matter who was unacquainted with the true situation. Here was a fresh obstacle in Peter's path. What should he do?

When he entered the ward he struggled bravely to bring his usual buoyancy to his command; but if the attempt was a sad failure it passed unnoticed, for the instant he came within sight Nat beckoned to him excitedly.

"Guess who's been to see me!" cried he, his eyes shining with the wonder of his tidings. "Guess, Peter! Oh, you never can guess--Mr. Coddington, the boss himself! Yes, he did," he repeated as he observed Peter's amazement. "He came this morning and he sat right in that chair--that very chair where you are sitting now. He wanted to know everything about the accident, and about you; I had to tell him about Mother and the rent, and how you were taking my place at home and paying for things while I was sick. He screwed it all out of me! He inquired just how much we paid for our rooms, and what I earned, and how long I had been in the beamhouse. Then he asked what Father's name was, and what Mother's family name was before she was married; and strangest of all, he wanted to know if we came from Orinville, Tennessee. That was my mother's old home, but I don't see how Mr. Coddington knew it, do you? Goodness, Peter! He shot off questions as if they were coming out of a gun. Then he began to ask about you and where you lived, and who your people were. Doesn't it seem funny, Pete--well as I know you I couldn't tell him one of those things? So I just said that I didn't know, but that Peter Strong was the finest fellow in the world, and he seemed to agree with me. Afterward he went away. What ever do you suppose made him come?"

"I don't know," Peter replied thoughtfully.

All the way home Peter pondered on the marvel. How had his father found out about his friendship for Nat? It must have been Bryant who had told; nobody else knew. Bryant had overheard Nat's conversation the day he had been taken to the hospital, and Bryant must have acquainted Mr. Coddington with the whole affair. Well, it was better so. His father now had the facts, and had them direct from Nat himself. Peter would be divulging no confidence if he mentioned them.

During the next few days many a surprise awaited Peter Strong. When he went to pay Mrs. Jackson's weekly rent he was told by the landlord that the account had already been settled, and the rent paid three months in advance. A gentleman had paid it. No, the landlord did not know who it was. In addition to this good fortune Mrs. Jackson astonished the boy still further by dangling before his gaze a substantial check which she said had come from the Coddington Company with a kind note of sympathy. The check was to be used for defraying expenses during the illness of her son.

Peter had no difficulty in guessing the source of this generosity.

Nor was this all. Nat scrawled him an incoherent note that bubbled with delight; he had been promoted to the finishing department, and henceforth was to receive a much larger salary!

That night Peter went home a very happy boy. It seemed as if there was not room for any more good things to be packed into a single day; but when at evening a crate came marked with his name, and on investigation it proved to contain the long-coveted motorcycle, Peter's joy knew no bounds.

"Do you suppose now that your chum Strong could let Peter Coddington return to school?" was his father's unexpected question.

Peter stopped short.

It was a long time before he spoke; then he said slowly:

"Father, I don't think there is a Peter Coddington any more. There's only Peter Strong, and he is so interested in his work and in doing real things that you couldn't coax him to go to school if you tried--especially since he has just been given a new motorcycle!"

Mr. Coddington rubbed his hands together as he always did when he was pleased.

"You must not decide hastily, Peter," urged he. "Take a week to think carefully about it and then tell me your decision."

"But I know now!" cried Peter. "A little while ago I thought the tannery the most awful place in the world; I hated the smell of it and the very sight of the leather. But somehow I do not feel that way now. I did not realize this until you spoke the other day of my leaving and going back to school; then I was surprised to discover that, when I thought it all over, I did not want to go back. Work can be fun--even hard work--if all the time you know that you are doing something real--something that is needed and that helps. If you don't mind, Father, I'd rather stay in the tannery and aid Peter Strong to work up."

"Do you still insist on Peter Strong's doing the climbing? Why not give Peter Coddington a chance?"

"I'd rather not, sir. It was Peter Strong who began at the foot of the ladder, and I want him to be the one to reach the top if he can; it is only fair. Please don't spoil it now by crowding Peter Coddington into his place."

"Well, well! You may do your own way, Peter, but it is on one condition. Nat Jackson needs a trip away. The doctors say he is tired out and won't get well as fast as he should unless he has a change of some sort. I am going to arrange with his mother to take him for a month to the seashore, and I know he will be much happier if Peter Strong goes with him. What do you say?"

Peter looked intently at his father, a tiny cloud darkening his face.

"You need not have any compunctions about going, Peter," explained Mr. Coddington, reading the trouble in his eyes. "Both the boys have worked faithfully and need a vacation. Their positions will be held for them until they return and their pay will go on during their absence."

"Oh, Father! How good of you to do so much, not only for me but for Nat and his mother!"

Mr. Coddington did not reply at once. After a pause he said gently:

"Peter, anything I can do for the Jackson family is but a small part of what I owe them. All my life I have tried to trace them. I have searched from Tennessee to Cape Cod. And now, here in my own tannery, I find the clue for which I have been hunting. Your friend Nat and his mother are proud people, and would never accept all that I wish I might offer them; but at least I have this opportunity to furnish help in a purely business way. To provide this trip is a great pleasure to me. Some time you shall know the whole story and then you will understand. I want you to know, for the obligation is one that will go down from father to son so long as a Coddington lives to bear the name. Good-night, my boy."

CHAPTER VII

THE CLIMB UP THE LADDER

If Peter expected to hear more of the mysterious tie that linked his family with that of the Jacksons he was disappointed; for his father did not refer to the story again, and although the boy burned with curiosity to know more he had not the courage to ask. Had not Mr. Coddington gone steadily forward perfecting plans for the seashore outing it would have seemed as if the incident had entirely slipped from his mind. But the personal interest he displayed in arranging every detail of the trip proved beyond question that the memory of the obligation at which he had hinted was still vividly before him. The vacation was arranged without trouble. Mrs. Jackson's first objections to accepting this favor at the hands of the Coddington Company were quieted when told by the doctors that the plan would be highly beneficial to the health of her boy. Both Peter and Nat were in high spirits. To lads who had been confined within doors all summer the prospect of bathing, sailing, and a month in the open was like water to the thirsty.

Fortunately Dame Nature herself smiled graciously upon the project, for during the next four weeks she coaxed back to earth warm, golden days from the fast fleeing Indian summer. The magic touch of sunshine and fresh air flooded Nat's cheek with healthy color and as if by miracle, strength returned to the delicate ankle; as for Peter he became swarthy as a young Arab. So delighted was Mrs. Jackson in watching the transformation in her two boys that she was quite unaware that a soft pinkiness was stealing into her own face. A vacation had seemed such an impossible thing that she had never dared picture how welcome such a rest would be.

When, weeks later, the trio returned to town and Mr. Coddington surprised them by meeting them at the station with the motor-car his gratification was extreme. He waved aside all thanks, however, and after dropping Nat and his mother at their home he rolled off with Peter, explaining that he would take the lad to his own door. Nat wondered not a little where that door was, and he would have been overwhelmed with amazement had he known that portals no less pretentious than those of the Coddington mansion itself opened to receive his chum. Very wide open indeed were they thrown when the car bringing Peter and his father turned into the long avenue leading to the house. How glad Peter's mother was to see him, and how satisfied she was with the witchcraft that wind and wave had wrought!

"I guess there is no doubt that now you are fit either for school or for work, Peter," said Mr. Coddington. "Which is it to be? Are you still firm in your decision to stick to the tannery? It isn't too late to change your mind, you know, if you wish to do so."

"I'm firmer for the tannery than ever, Father," answered Peter, smiling.

"Going to fight it out, are you?"

"Yes, sir."

"Good!"

It was only one word, but Peter knew that his father was pleased.

Accordingly on the following Monday morning the boy again took up his old work in the finishing department. Here Nat joined him, and since this branch of leather manufacture was an entirely new world to Jackson, Peter took his turn at explaining its various processes, and felt no little pride in having the teaching obligations reversed, and being able to give his chum instructions concerning matters of which he was ignorant. The two boys were becoming quite expert at boarding calfskins and had settled down with great contentment to this task when one day they were surprised and perhaps not a little disappointed to receive orders to leave their present occupation and report for duty at Factory 2, the sheepskin tannery.

[Illustration: IN THE FINISHING DEPARTMENT]

"Another beamhouse!" exclaimed Peter in dismay. "I thought we were through with that sort of thing for good and all, Nat."

"Oh, it isn't likely we'll stay there," was Nat's hopeful rejoinder. "Evidently somebody higher up wants us to have this chance to see how sheepskins are prepared and I, for one, am not sorry for I've no very clear idea."

"I'm worse off than you, Nat," chuckled Peter. "I've no idea at all."

"Nonsense, Peter! By this time you must know the general process for preparing skins."

"Why, yes. I suppose the hair is taken off and the skins tanned just as calfskins are."

"Yes, the main facts are the same. There are many points, however, where the processes differ because the skins of sheep, kids, goats, and such creatures must undergo entirely different treatment. The kid used for gloves and even for shoes, you see, is far more delicate than is the calfskin that we have been finishing."

"Yes, of course," agreed Peter thoughtfully. "Well, I suppose we shall now find out all about it and that it will be interesting; but I do wish, Nat, that we could learn it somewhere except in another beamhouse."

Peter's wish, alas, was of no avail and accordingly once more the two boys donned rubber boots and overalls and started again at the foot of the ladder-- this time in Factory 2, where the skins of sheep, kids, and goats were tanned. Sheepskins, they soon learned, were received by the tanners in one of two conditions: either the wool was already off and they arrived in casks drenched or pickled, many bales of one dozen each being packed in a cask; or the skins came to the tannery salted, with the wool on and precisely in the condition that they were when taken from the backs of the sheep at the ranches and abattoirs. So long as the hair was on the skins were called "pelts"; but the moment the hair was removed the skins became "slats." The pickled skins it was simple enough to tan, for they had been carefully prepared for the tanners before being shipped; there were firms, the foreman told Peter, that did just this very thing. If desired the pickled sheepskins could even be worked into a cheap white leather without further tanning. Most of them, however, were tanned.

But the unhairing of the sheep pelts was a different problem. After they had been soaked about twenty-four hours in borax and water to get out the dirt and salt they must first be put through a machine that cleansed the wool and shaved off any fat adhering to the flesh side. Then they were ready to have the wool removed. A very delicate process this was, Peter and Nat soon discovered. Each pelt was spread smoothly on a table wool side down, and a preparation of lime and sulphide of sodium was spread evenly over it with a brush, great care being taken to let none of the liquid used get upon the wool side of the skin. The pelt was then folded and left from eight to ten hours until the solution which had been brushed over it had penetrated it and loosened the hair. The wool could then very easily be pulled off, sorted as the skins were unhaired, and sold to dealers as "pulled wool."

One fact interested Peter very much, and that was that usually the slats were thinnest where the wool was longest.

"I suppose the strength of the sheep all went to its hair," speculated he to Nat. "Isn't it funny that it should!"

Another thing the boys learned about sheepskins which was very different from the treatment of calfskins was that before the slats could be tanned they had to be put through a powerful press and have the grease squeezed out of them.

"The skin of a sheep has a vast amount of oil in it," explained one of the workmen, "and it is impossible to do anything until this grease has been extracted; so we put a bunch of skins under a heavy press and then collect the grease that runs out, refine, and sell it."

Peter and Nat watched this pressing with great interest.

When the skins came out of the press they were so hard and stiff that it was necessary to put them into the revolving drums that separated and softened them. This was called "wheeling up the slats." The odor in the press room was far worse than anything that Peter had yet encountered--much more disagreeable than was an ordinary beamhouse. Both he and Nat were only too glad when noon time came and they could get out into the air.

"Whew!" cried Peter, throwing himself down in the sunshine, "I hope they don't put us in that press room to work, Nat."

"It's fierce, isn't it?" Nat answered. "The men must hate it."

"I suppose they get accustomed to it just as I got used to the beamhouse," Peter said. "Why, when I began work in the beamhouse of Factory 1 I thought I never could endure it. Do you remember how you tried to cheer me up that first day?"

Nat laughed at the memory.

"Indeed I do. You looked perfectly hopeless, Peter."

"That's about the way I felt," smiled Peter, "and I believe I'd feel so again if I thought I had weeks of that press room smell before me."

But Peter need not have feared any such calamity, for after lunch he and Nat were given a lesson in tanning sheepskins and were told they were to work at that task until further notice.

The process, they discovered, differed very radically from the calfskin treatment with which they were so familiar. Many of the slats were tanned by being laid in trays of fine, moist powder that looked like brown sugar.

"What is this stuff?" inquired Peter of a man who stood near by.

"That is sumac, young man."

"Sumac! Just common sumac?"

"Well, no. It is the same sort of thing, though. We import this from Sicily, because the foreign leaves grow larger and contain more tannin. Sicilian sumac makes better leather than does the American variety, which comes chiefly from Virginia."

Peter nodded.

"And how long, pray, do the skins lie covered up in this snuffy brown powder?" questioned Nat.

"About a week," answered the man. "We do not tan all sheepskins this way, however. Some, as you will see, are tanned by being suspended from a bar into a vat of quebracho. Others are put into wheels of chrome tan just as calfskins are. White leathers are tanned, or more properly speaking tawed, in a mixture of alum and egg-yolk."

"Egg-yolk!" gasped Peter. "Eggs--such as we eat?"

"I am not so sure that they are such as you would care to eat," grinned the man, "but the yolks come from eggs, nevertheless."

"I should think it would take lots of men to break the eggs fast enough and get them ready," murmured Peter, half aloud.

"Bless your heart! We don't break the eggs here!" roared the workman, shaking with laughter. "No, indeed. We get egg-yolk by the barrel; when we pour it out it looks like thin yellow paint. We tan kid for gloves in egg-yolk," he went on, observing that both Nat and Peter were much interested. "After sheepskins are tanned the leather must all be fat-liquored, dried by steam or air fans, dampened, split or shaved off to uniform thickness, dyed in revolving paddle-wheels filled with color, and tacked on boards to dry just as calfskins are. The chemists who have laboratories up-stairs test the dyes and mix or match the colors for us. Then the skins go to the various rooms for the different finishes. And speaking of finishes, I suppose you went into the buffing-room in the other factory."

"No," said Peter, "we didn't--at least I didn't."

"Nor I," put in Nat. "The door was always closed and no one was admitted."

"They don't like to have people go in if they can help it because every time the door is opened it stirs things up; but I can take you into our buffing-room if you want to go."

"I wish you would," cried Peter.

Accordingly all went up-stairs and their guide cautiously pushed open a door on which NO ADMITTANCE was scrawled in large letters. The moment Peter squeezed through it he drew in his breath and then regretted that he had done so, for he at once began to cough.

The boys glanced about the room before them.

Every window was closed, making the air hot and stuffy; yet, Peter asked himself, how was such a condition to be avoided in a place where it was evident that even the tiniest draught must create instant havoc? This room which Peter and Nat surveyed was thick with flying white particles that were being whirled into space from rapidly turning emery wheels. The workmen who were busy buffing the flesh side of split skins in order to get the rough surface required for a suede finish seemed enveloped in a miniature blizzard. As the swiftly turning discs sent clouds of white dust into the air it settled on the hair, faces, eyelashes, and clothing until the laborers looked like snow men moving amid the blinding flakes of an old-fashioned storm. Peter and Nat, who looked on, began to be changed into snow men, too.

"I guess you don't want to stay in here long," announced their guide, raising his voice to be heard above the noise of the revolving wheels. "As you see, they are making 'suede,' or ooze finished leather. Some calfskins are finished this way too, as of course you know. A certain amount of this leather will be left white for gloves or shoes; more of it, however, will be stretched on boards and brushed over with some colored dye. Suede is made in all sorts of fancy shades for women's party slippers."

Peter nodded and then, quite without warning, he sneezed.

Immediately a cloud of whiteness shot into the air.

"Hurry! Let's get out!" cried Nat. "I'm going to sneeze, too."

The man who was conducting them opened the door a crack and they all three slipped through. Safe in the outer room they stopped and laughingly surveyed one another. All were as white as if sprinkled with powder.

"Goodness!" Peter exclaimed, rubbing his eyelashes. "How can those men breathe? I should think that in a day they would swallow enough dust to fill their lungs up solid."

"They don't mind it."

"Well, I only hope we shan't be put in there to work."

"So do I!" was Nat's fervent rejoinder.

Fortunately for the boys they escaped doing duty in the buffing-room. Instead they worked throughout the year in the beamhouse and the different finishing departments of Factory 2. Although this factory was known as the sheepskin tannery they soon found that the skins of lambs, kids, and goats were also tanned and finished there. The skins of the young kids or goats were much too delicate for shoes and were made into thin flexible leather for kid gloves; the leather commonly known as kid and used for shoes was not really kid at all, the boys were told, but the skin of mature goats. Inquiry also brought forth the surprising information that there were between sixty and seventy different kinds of goatskin, the thickness and grain of the material depending on the climate and the conditions under which the animals had been raised. Some of these skins were imported from Brazil, some from Buenos Ayres, Mexico, France, Russia, India, China, Tripoli, or Arabia.

Goat breeders, the foreman said, killed their flocks at the season of the year when the men who collected skins made their rounds. These collectors went from one station to another and the goat herders, carrying bundles of skins on their backs, went down to the station nearest the hill country in which they were grazing their flocks and sold their stock to the collector, who promptly paid them in cash. When the collector had bought all the skins he wished he had them baled and sent them across country to the nearest seaport from which they were shipped to America. Many of the skins coming from India and Russia were sent first to London and then reshipped to the United States.

All goatskins, of no matter what variety, were tanned by the chrome process, and because they were smaller and of lighter weight than hides, tanned much more quickly. They were finished in many different ways: glazed kid, which was made in colors as well as black, had a shiny surface made by "striking" or burnishing the leather on the grain side; mat kid, soft and dull, was treated with oil and wax; suede kid was made in fancy colors for party shoes. These were some of the most important varieties. Then there was buckskin, the skin of the reindeer, most frequently buffed and finished in colors for gloves, or in white for shoes. Kangaroo was also classed under the head of kid.

"Is patent kid finished in this factory?" inquired Peter one day.

"No. All the patent leathers--both patent kid and patent calf--have a factory all to themselves."

"I'd like to see it."

"Oh, you will some day, no doubt. I hear they need a new boss over there. The men hate Tolman. Who knows but you may get his job!"

Peter laughed, and so did the other men who chanced to be standing about.

"I guess there is no danger that Tolman will lose his place on my account," replied the boy with no little amusement.

Many months later when Peter met Tolman he recalled this incident and understood more fully why the men disliked him and felt that the patent leather factory needed a new head.

CHAPTER VIII

A NARROW ESCAPE AND ITS CONSEQUENCES

All this time, strangely enough, no hint of Peter Strong's identity had become known. It was little short of a miracle that it should not have been discovered. Many circumstances, however, fostered the secret. In the first place none of the men from the tanneries ever came to the fashionable west side of the town; there was nothing to call them there. Had they come the chances were that they would probably at some time have encountered Peter in company with his father and mother driving, motoring, or going to church. Several school friends had, it is true, unearthed the interesting information that Peter was "working," but the discovery was greeted with but scant curiosity. One's place in life closes up very quickly after one drops from sight. When the idol of the Milburn ball team had vanished it had caused great agitation and for a brief interval he had been sincerely mourned; then some one else had been raised up to fill the gap, life was readjusted, and soon Peter and his glorious record were forgotten.

Under other conditions this lack of loyalty on the part of his friends would have wounded Peter sorely; now, however, the feeling was one of mortified pride rather than pained regret. His own attitude toward his former comrades had also in the meantime undergone a change. The boys he had looked up to, even the wisest of the seniors, seemed to him very young indeed, and their football worries pitiably unimportant. They were but preparing for the real work of the world while Peter, and others like him, were actually doing it. In consequence not a lad among all his former classmates was half so companionable or congenial as was his new friend, Nat Jackson.

And so, as the months sped past and Peter's second year in the tannery neared its end, he found himself not only content with the present life but more and more absorbed in each fresh experience of leather making. The bond with the Jackson home strengthened, and the desire to make good at his "job" drove him to throw all the interest and power of his strong young life into his task.

Winter had added many facts to his growing knowledge about leather. Up to February he and Nat had been together in the beamhouse and seen the great care which was taken that the freshly tanned skins should not freeze. Fortunately for the Coddington Company most of their buildings were new and were equipped with steam-heated lofts where drying could be accomplished with little trouble; but one or two of the old buildings had shutters and in consequence were dependent upon drying the wet skins in the outer air. If the leather was allowed to freeze its fibre was greatly weakened and its value decreased. Accordingly during cold weather the shutters in the old factories had to be closed and the newly tanned hides piled on the floor and covered with heavy canvas. Of course the leather rolled badly, but since it was possible to dampen and stretch it into shape this difficulty could be overcome.

In the finishing department where the two lads were next sent many more new features swelled their increasing fund of information. Wherever they went they left a train of friends behind them. Peter seemed to be the general property of the tanneries. The men quarreled good-naturedly over which factory could really claim the Little Giant. To all this chaff Peter returned modest replies and the odd little chuckle that had so endeared him to his schoolmates. Nobody could imitate that chuckle--nobody--although many of them tried. It was a part of Peter himself, a part of the good will he felt toward the world and everybody in it.

"You can't hear it without your heart warming toward the lad," remarked Carmachel one day.

Armed with this simple weapon Peter went on his way. He met the men about him with a frank expectation that they would like him, and they did. Nat also made friends, but as he was a much quieter boy most of those who sought him out did so because he shone with a glory reflected from Peter. Was he not Strong's chum? He must somehow be worth knowing if he had that honor.

This rough kindliness of the workmen robbed labor of much of its hardship. The two lads pushed eagerly ahead and were delighted when, toward spring, they were again promoted--this time to the department which turned out the tooled and embossed leathers.

This was one of the most fascinating phases of leather making and for a long time it had interested both Peter and Nat. It seemed too good to be true that they should now win positions in that factory.

"It's like the stories of the Arabian Nights, the way we've gone on and all the time kept together, Peter," Nat said one day. "Think of it! We have been given more money and better jobs all the time. I do not just see why, either. Lots of the men who started long ago in the beamhouse of Factory 1 are still there and haven't had a cent added to their pay envelope; and look at us! It's just luck-- that's what it is."

"Not entirely luck, Nat," objected Peter, shaking his head. "Some of it, to be sure, is sheer good fortune; but some of it is hard work. If we had not made good every step of the way I doubt if we should have been sent on up the ladder."

"I wonder!" was Nat's thoughtful answer. "Do you know, Pete, I've sometimes thought that perhaps Mr. Coddington was keeping an eye on us and giving orders that we be shoved along. He could do it, I suppose, if he wanted to."

"I suppose he could," agreed Peter, uneasily, "but he is pretty busy, and is it likely----"

"No, of course it isn't. He did a lot for me when I was sick and it isn't reasonable to think he would do anything more. He wouldn't be called upon to. It is just that we are under a lucky star."

"I wish the star was a lucky enough one to send you a motorcycle then, Nat," laughed Peter. "You know this going off riding by myself is no sort of a stunt. I don't have any fun at all. Why, I would rather tramp the country on my two feet with you than to ride all over it without you. Somehow you've got to get a motorcycle, Nat--you've simply got to."

"And just how do you expect me to carry out such a crazy scheme?" was the derisive retort. "Maybe you've a plan to suggest whereby, entirely without a cent, I am to purchase a toy like that. It can't be done without Aladdin's lamp-- at least I can't do it any other way. A motorcycle indeed! Why, I have not a cent to spend for such a thing. I couldn't even buy one of the pedals, let alone anything more. Forget it, Peter, and let's talk sense."

"I shan't forget it," Peter answered earnestly. "You are going to have a motorcycle if I have to--to--pawn my rubber boots to get you one."

They both laughed.

Peter was in great spirits.

This was their first day in the new factory and as the boys took up the novel task of learning how to make embossed leathers he made the inward resolve that every penny he earned there should be put into the bank toward a motorcycle for Nat.

The embossing department was indeed a wonderful place. Such magic as was wrought here! Pieces of dyed leather of every imaginable hue were put into great machines where heavy squares of copper, set in powerful presses, stamped upon them various patterns or impressions. The designs engraved on the dies were imitations of the texture of every known sort of fancy leather. There was alligator, lizard skin, pigskin, snakeskin and sealskin; even grained leather was copied. So perfect was the likeness that it seemed impossible to tell the embossed and artificially made material from the real.

"How is any one to know whether his card-case is real seal or not?" queried Peter, aghast at the perfection of the dies.

The foreman shrugged his shoulders.

"I guess you'd have some trouble," said he. "Comfort yourself, though, that you are not the only one. Just this fall Mr. Coddington himself came in here to compare our leather with some pieces of seal he had had sent him. He put his samples down on the table and later on when he went to get them he could not tell for the life of him which they were. We had a great laugh about it, I can tell you. Yes, we do pretty good work here, and we have about all the orders for pocketbook and bag leather that we can fill. At present we are so busy that we are running all the dies, and that is why we need extra men."

Peter and Nat found that the department was indeed busy. All day they were upon their feet feeding pieces of leather into the presses, and it was their fatigue--a fact unimportant in itself--which led to a remarkable chain of events in the Coddington tanneries.

It happened that one morning Peter was sent up to the shipping room on the sixth floor of the factory with a bale of finished leather, and when he was ready to return he found that the elevator which he had used in coming up was out of order, and that he must now walk down the many flights of stairs. Accordingly he started, whistling as he went. When he reached the fifth floor he was much surprised to discover that it was vacant. A great expanse it was, flooded with sunshine. Peter paused to look about. Some unused packing-cases littered one corner of the room and instantly the thought flashed into his mind--what a warm, quiet, secluded spot for him and Nat to eat their lunch! Why, they could even bring a book and curl up in the shelter of the boxes and read. As it was still too chilly to go out there was no way, during the winter months, but to huddle somewhere under the machinery of the factory and eat one's lunch. Peter detested the arrangement, unavoidable as it was, and always rejoiced when the noon hour was over.

But here was an escape from such disagreeable conditions. Here was an unused room! Why should it not become a refuge from the noise, the dirt, and the turmoil of the factory? The plan seemed innocent enough, and when Peter confided it to Nat neither of them could see the slightest objection to it. In consequence, at noon time they crept up-stairs, and arranged a cozy little corner for themselves behind the packing-cases. It was almost as good as playing Robinson Crusoe, this building a fortress and hiding inside it. Then, too, the constant chance of being discovered provided just the necessary tremor of excitement to make it interesting. What fun it was! They called their stronghold Sterling Castle, and many a joke and jibe they made concerning it--jokes at which they laughed heartily when they were by themselves.

The vast empty space, they learned by cautious questioning, had originally been intended as a supply room; it was found, however, that it was not needed for this purpose and therefore it had been left in its present unoccupied condition.

There seemed not an iota of possibility that the place would ever be used and Peter and Nat exulted in the fact that they might lunch there undisturbed for the rest of their days if they so desired. For weeks they spent every noon hour in the sunshine behind their barricade talking softly together, eating their luncheon, and sometimes reading aloud.

Then came calamity.

It was on a sharp April day when the shelter of their sunny corner was especially welcome. Peter had just been rolling out one of the most stirring chapters of "Ivanhoe" when suddenly he paused, listening intently.

"It's the elevator!" he whispered. "It is stopping at this floor. Somebody is getting out, Nat."

"Who can it be?"

"Hush!"

The two boys kept very still.

Steps and voices came nearer.

"Yes, every floor is protected by fire-escapes, as you see," declared a voice.

"It is some insurance man," breathed Peter. "Don't move, Nat."

"Have you hand extinguishers here also?"

"Yes, at each corner of the room and on the walls."

"This floor is not in use, I take it."

"No," broke in another voice--the voice of Mr. Coddington himself. "We never have had occasion to use this floor, although we probably shall do so when we require more room for supplies. What are those packing-cases doing here, Tyler? They look as though they were empty."

"I hardly think empty cases would be left on this floor, sir. They shouldn't be."

Mr. Tyler was evidently annoyed.

"Empty or full, they've no business in this room," said Mr. Coddington, sharply. "They might cause fire."

Simultaneously the three men stepped forward to investigate.

Mr. Tyler kicked the back of the nearest case with his foot, but Mr. Coddington, who never stopped until he had got at the bottom of things, grasped the edge of one of the great boxes and tried to turn it over.

Now it happened that the boys, struggling to remain unseen, had huddled into this very box.

"The case is heavy, Tyler. I can't stir it. Just see what is in it."

Mr. Tyler, alert to obey, dragged forth the case with the assistance of the insurance agent and when it was tipped up and Peter and Nat tumbled out on the floor three more astonished men never were seen.

[Illustration: THE THREE MEN STEPPED FORWARD]

"How did you two boys get here?" questioned Mr. Tyler severely. "What are you doing?"

Nat, thoroughly terrified, looked helplessly at Peter. He couldn't have answered had he tried. Peter himself was a good deal taken aback. He glanced at his father for some hint as to how to proceed, but Mr. Coddington's face was a study in conflicting emotions and furnished no clue. Therefore, after waiting a moment and receiving no aid in his dilemma, Peter replied simply:

"We are eating our luncheon."

"Eating your lunch! And who told you you might come here for such a purpose?"

"Nobody. It just was a big, empty place with lots of sunshine and it seemed nicer than eating down-stairs," gasped Peter.

"Are you sure they were eating their lunch and not starting a fire?" suggested the insurance inspector in an undertone.

"Of course we weren't setting a fire!" Peter cried indignantly, hearing the whispered words of the inspector. "We just came up here to get where it was clean and quiet. When it is too cold to go out there isn't any place to eat except right in the factory."

"Well, that is no excuse for your coming here. It is against the rule for any of the employees to come above the fourth floor without permission. I thought you both understood that. If you didn't it is your own fault. You may finish out your week here and on Saturday night you may consider yourselves discharged from the tannery." Mr. Tyler put his hand on Peter's shoulder. "I'm sorry, Strong," he added.

"Just one moment, Tyler."

It was Mr. Coddington who spoke.

"Tell me more fully about this matter, Peter Strong. You say you have no suitable place to eat your lunch."

"Yes, sir."

"What do the other men do?"

"They sit around under the machinery anywhere they can. Often the place is dirty and sometimes it is hot. If the windows are opened to air the rooms the men get cold," answered Peter.

"Strong is a little fussy, I am afraid, Mr. Coddington," interrupted Mr. Tyler. "The conditions are the same as they always have been--the same as they are in most mills. The men can go home at noon if they like."

"But they can't get home, and eat anything, and get back here, all within an hour," objected Peter. "Besides, they are often too tired. It is much easier to stay right in the tannery. Of course in warm weather we have the park and can go outside, so then we are all right; but during the winter----"

"That will do, Strong," cut in Mr. Tyler. "Remember your time is up this week. What's your name?" The superintendent turned severely on Nat.

"Jackson."

"Oh, yes--Jackson. You are the boy who was hurt."

Nat nodded.

"I am sorry to see that you are making such a poor return to the company for its kindness to you. It is unfortunate all around. But we cannot have the rules of the tannery broken. Mr. Coddington will, I am sure, agree with me there."

"Undoubtedly, Tyler. Any person who is at fault should be punished. In this particular case, however, just who *is* at fault? If, as the lads say, they have nowhere to go at noon, is the fault wholly theirs if they seek a remedy from their discomfort? Suppose we suspend their sentence until we investigate the conditions and simply caution them not to repeat the offense. Had these empty cases not been left here by some negligent persons seclusion would have been impossible. Somebody beside the boys was to blame. Order the boxes removed and drop the matter."

Without another word Mr. Coddington stalked toward the elevator and the men who accompanied him had no choice but to follow.

Peter and Nat breathed a sigh of relief.

There had been but a hair's breadth between them and a discharge from the tannery! To Peter the danger was not a very real one, but Nat, who was in ignorance of the true facts, was pale with fright.

"Whew, Peter! That was a close call," he stammered. "A narrow squeak! But for Mr. Coddington we should both have been fired. I don't know what I should have done if I had lost my place. It was mighty good of him to give us another chance, wasn't it?"

"Mr. Coddington is all right, you can bet your life on that!" agreed Peter heartily. "It was lucky, though, that he was here."

Still aglow with excitement, the boys flew down over the stairs and took up their work, making no further allusion to the incident.

But that night when Peter got home his father called him into the library and motioning to a chair before the open fire, observed dryly:

"Your friend Strong had a narrow escape to-day, Peter."

"Yes, sir. But for you he would have lost his job."

"I'm afraid so," the president nodded. "Since noon I have been thinking the matter over. What Strong said brought things before me in an entirely new light. I don't think I ever realized before some of the conditions at the tanneries."

Peter waited.

"If it were possible--mind, I do not say it could be done--but if a scheme could be worked out to make a big sort of rest room where the men could go at noon do you think that would obviate the difficulties of my employees? Would it prevent them from converting packing-cases into lunch rooms?"

"You mean a big room with tables and chairs where the men could go and eat their lunch, Father?"

"Something of the sort. Perhaps there could be magazines and books there, too."

"Hurrah! It's a splendid plan. When will you do it, Father?" cried Peter.

"I didn't say I was going to do it at all. I merely asked you to find out your friend Strong's opinion. Do you know, some of Strong's ideas are not so bad. Ask him if a room such as I describe would be as satisfactory to him as the packing-box lunch room from which he and his friend Jackson were to-day ejected."

"Of course Strong will like it!"

"I think I will give the orders, then. That vacant floor may as well be used for this purpose as any other. We shall not want it at present, and if we ever need more room we must devise some other way. I've a fancy, somehow, to call the new venture the Strong Reading-Room."

Peter started to speak.

"Purely as a joke, you know," went on Mr. Coddington, waving his hand. "Just as a reminder to Strong how very near he came to losing his position."

Mr. Coddington glanced up humorously; then he chuckled and so did Peter.

CHAPTER IX

PETER AIDS IN A SURPRISE AND RECEIVES ONE

All the next few months corps of men worked secretly transforming into a reading-room the great vacant place, which, on that memorable day, Peter and Nat had appropriated as a lunch room. Carpenters laid the new floor and stained it; painters tinted the walls a soft green; masons constructed a hospitable fireplace. One end of the room was furnished with tiers of book-shelves, tables, chairs, and reading lights; the other was dotted with a myriad of small tables for the use of those who wished to lunch at the factories.

Then one Sunday afternoon when everything was completed Peter and his father made a clandestine trip to the tannery and admitting themselves, crept up-stairs where Mr. Coddington unlocked the door of the "forbidden chamber." The whole room glowed with sunshine which flooded the polished floors and reflected its brightness in the shiny brass andirons adorning the fireplace.

Peter, who had not seen the place since it was finished, exclaimed with delight.

"You are satisfied then, Peter?" inquired his father, enjoying his pleasure. "Do you think there is anything else that your friend Strong would suggest?"

The lad looked critically about.

"Only one thing, and perhaps that is not necessary after all. But doesn't it seem to you that the space over the fireplace needs a picture or something? It looks so bare!"

"A picture! I had not thought of that. Yes, I see what you mean."

"Just one picture," went on Peter. "Something that will show well from this end of the room when people come in."

"Yes, it would certainly be a distinct improvement. We'll have a picture there."

Peter raised his eyes shyly to his father's face.

"I think it would be nice," he said, "to have a picture of you."

"A picture of me! Pooh, pooh! Nonsense! The men see me often enough--too often, I fancy. Remember they do not care for me as you do. No, indeed! I could not think of sticking my own portrait up in my tanneries. I shouldn't want to see it myself."

"I don't suppose you would," admitted Peter, reluctantly.

"But we'll have a picture there all the same, Peter. Will you trust me to select it?"

"Of course I will. Just get something to do with sheep or horses--something that the men will enjoy and understand."

Mr. Coddington smiled down into the eager face.

"I guess I can find a picture the men will like; it may take a little while, though, to get just the right thing. Had we better throw open the room now without it, or wait until everything is complete?"

"Oh, wait! Wait!" was Peter's plea. "Do not open it until everything is done! We do not need to use the place at this season of the year anyway, because the weather is now so warm that every one goes to the park at noon. The secret can be kept until fall, can't it?"

"Yes, indeed. Nobody, with the exception of Mr. Tyler and the workmen, knows about the room; and they are pledged not to tell."

Accordingly the shades of the new reading-room were lowered, it was securely locked, and the key put into Mr. Coddington's pocket.

As the hammering that had for so long echoed through the factory ceased queries concerning the noise and the mission of the carpenters died away. Even Peter himself forgot about the great mystery, for the ball season was now on and in addition to its engrossing interests he and Nat were transferred to Factory 3 where they became much absorbed in the tanning of cowhides. Here again the preparation of the leather took them back to the beamhouse with its familiar processes of liming, unhairing, puering and tanning. Was there never to be an end to beamhouses, Peter wondered.

"No sooner do we get out of one and find ourselves happy at some clean, decent work than off we go to another! I am about tired of beamhouses!" wailed Peter.

Nevertheless the two boys stuck resolutely to the beamhouse and to tanning cowhides.

At Factory 3 there also were tanned other light weight hides that underwent a chrome process of tannage rather than the oak or hemlock processes used at the sole leather plant at Elmwood.

It seemed to Peter that he had never dreamed there were so many creatures in the whole world until he began to handle the shipments of hides that came to the factory to be tanned.

"Do all these skins come from the ranches of our own country?" he inquired one day when, from the window, he saw a train of heavily laden freight cars come rolling into the yard. "Why, I shouldn't think there would be a single live animal left in America."

"There wouldn't," replied the boss good-naturedly. "No, indeed. Only a small part of the hides tanned here and at the Elmwood tanneries come from our ranches. The United States cannot begin to produce hides enough to fill the demand. Therefore we import a great many from abroad as well as from South America. When a shipment arrives the skins are sorted: the cowhides and those to be tanned in chrome coming here, and the heavy skins and those to be tanned in oak or hemlock being sent on to Elmwood, where all the sole leather is made. The hides vary in weight, ranging from twenty-five to sixty pounds. There are skins of steers, horses, buffaloes, walrus, bulls, and oxen. The strongest and most perfect ones are made into belting to run the machinery of factories. Leather for this purpose, as you can easily see, must be of equal strength in every part to withstand the great strain put upon it. Some factories turn out belting and nothing else. Other heavy hides are tanned into sole leather for harnesses, bags, trunks, and the soles of shoes. Then there are lots of hides which are not perfect. These are the skins of branded cattle and steers. You know, of course, that on many of the ranches the stock is branded so that it can be easily identified in case it is lost. These branded hides have flaws or thin places in them and are not so valuable in consequence."

"I can see that," assented Peter. "What is done with such leather?"

"Well, it is usually tanned in oak, or in a blend of oak and hemlock known as union tan, and is sold for purposes where less strength will be demanded of it than if it were made into belting."

Peter nodded.

"Oh, there are lots of interesting things to learn about hides. Why, you wouldn't believe, now would you, that the way the animals live would make a difference in the weight of their skins? Yet it is so. Cattle raised in stalls and supplied regularly with good food have far better hides than those that range the fields and are forced to forage for the scant rations found there. Wild cattle, on the other hand, have much tougher hides than do domesticated animals."

"It's curious, isn't it?" replied Peter.

"Yes, it is," the foreman answered. "Two factors always go hand in hand in the making of a fine leather. One is the quality of the hide itself; and the other is the way in which it is tanned. For the tanning liquid, you know, reacts on the fibres of the skin in such a way that the material becomes tougher, closer grained, and more pliable. Here again you are back to the importance of the beamhouse processes."

All these items of information Peter and Nat added to their accumulating fund. Through the long summer they worked hard, classifying all they learned and collecting more as one gathers up snow by rolling a snowball.

Then came the fall, with its frosts of ever increasing heaviness. The park flowers drooped; baseball failed to drive the cold from chilled fingers; and lunching in the open had to be abandoned. It was then that notices were posted in all the tanneries saying that at noon on a certain day the president of the Coddington Company desired to meet his men in the vacant room of Factory 2.

Peter's heart beat high!

At last the secret of the reading-room was to be made public!

Would the men like their new quarters, he wondered. What an absurd speculation! Of course they would.

Yet it was not without some anxiety that, in company with Nat, Peter made his way to Factory 2 the moment the noon whistle blew on that great day. A tide of workmen moved hither with him. On every hand they poured in through the doors and streamed up the stairways. The two boys followed. Everybody was speculating as to what the president could want. Then, as the vanguard of the crowd reached the fifth floor, Peter heard a rush of sound--cheers and cries of surprise. The mystery, so long guarded, stood revealed!

A lump rose in the lad's throat. The men were pleased, and his father, who had spent so much time and money on the carrying out of this project, would consider himself more than repaid for all he had done. Poor Peter! He almost felt personally responsible that the men should appreciate his father's kindness. So anxious had he been that had those hundreds of voices not risen with just the spontaneity they did it would have broken his heart. But the cheers swelled from the scores of throats with a heartiness not to be questioned.

Silently he and Nat pushed their way into the crowded room. Far away in the glow of a blazing fire Peter could see his father, wreathed in smiles, talking with Mr. Tyler. And it was just at that moment that the boy remembered about the picture which was to have been purchased and raised his eyes curiously to the space over the fireplace. To his chagrin the spot was covered with a piece of green cambric. The picture his father had promised to buy had not come! For a fraction of a second Peter sobered with disappointment; then in the excitement of the cheering he forgot all about it.

In answer to shouts and cheers Mr. Coddington stepped forward and raised his hand.

There was instant stillness.

"It gives me great pleasure to see that you like the room," said he, simply, "and I am grateful to you for so heartily expressing your approval. But before we go further I feel it is only honest to confess to you that it is neither the Coddington Company nor myself that you should thank for this new library. Shall I tell you how you chanced to have it?"

"Yes! Yes!" came from all over the room.

Then in humorous fashion Mr. Coddington sketched the tale of two boys and an interrupted luncheon, drawing a vivid picture of how the lads had been unceremoniously tumbled to the floor out of their stronghold in the packing-boxes. Mr. Coddington had a gift for telling a story and he told this one with consummate skill.

At its conclusion there was a general laugh.

"Those boys are with us to-day," continued the president. "They are not strangers to you. One of them is Nat Jackson, whom you all know well, and the other--the lad who furnished me with the inspiration for this venture is----"

Instantly the curtain over the fireplace was withdrawn.

"Peter Strong!" cried the men.

It was indeed Peter who smiled down on the throng from out the broad gilt frame! Not Peter Coddington of the fashionable "west side,"--the son and heir of the president of the company, but Peter Strong--Peter in faded jumper and with the collar of his shirt turned away so that one could see where the firm young head rose out of it; Peter with hair tumbled, cheeks flushed from hard work, and his eyes shining as they always shone when he was happy; Peter Strong--the Peter the men knew and loved!

The boy himself looked on, bewildered. Well he knew the source of the portrait. It had evidently been copied from a snap-shot Nat had taken of him one day when the two were coming out of the beamhouse. His father's delay in finding a suitable picture was also now explained. He had had to wait for the portrait to be painted.

Nat, who was watching Peter's face with no small degree of amusement, now whispered:

"I kept one secret from you anyhow, Peter. Mr. Coddington came to see us one evening last spring and asked if I had any kodak picture of you, explaining what he wanted it for. So I let him look over what I had and he chose this one. It's fine, isn't it?"

"Why, I don't know," stammered Peter. "I--I'm so flabbergasted I----"

Nat laughed.

All this time the men were cheering and now cries of "Peter Strong!" "Peter Strong!" rent the air.

The unlucky Peter, who was vainly trying to flatten himself against the wall and hide in Nat's shadow, was dragged forth by Carmachel and made to stand upon a table, from which elevation he waved his hand to the men and then, ducking suddenly, buried himself once more in the crowd.

After waiting a little while for the tumult to subside Mr. Coddington again began to speak--this time in a low, uncertain voice:

"I see you all recognize the portrait. It is Peter Strong as you have met and known him. Yet we can never tell what the future will unfold. If it chanced that time should bring to this lad a career fraught with greater responsibilities than he now holds I want you to remember that he came into the works a boy, like many of you; that he was one with you in play as well as in work; that he toiled at the hardest tasks, never shunning what was difficult or disagreeable; that he was, is, and I hope will always be, your comrade--the product of the Coddington tanneries."

With a bow and a smile to the silent crowd before him the president withdrew. Then as the workmen turned to disperse a few clear words from some one in the throng behind caught Peter's ear:

"It's more than likely the president means to push Strong along to the top of the ladder. He is mightily interested in the boy; anybody can see that. Mayhap the lad will make up to him for his own son who, I've heard say, is a lazy little snob and a great disappointment to his father."

CHAPTER X

THE CLIMB BECOMES DIFFICULT

It would not have been strange if with all this adulation Peter had come to think himself a very clever boy--perhaps the cleverest one in the world. Fortunately for his modesty, however, his daily life did not tend to foster any such delusion. He received occasional commendation, it is true, from his superiors, but to counterbalance it he continued to have many a rebuke thrown at him during the year he and Nat toiled together tanning hides. The newness of the work combined with a score of well-meant blunders placed Peter Strong on entirely equal footing with other workmen, and quite as liable to correction. Even had these conditions been otherwise the memory of the lazy little snob who was a great disappointment to his father would have served to crush in the lad any undue sense of his own importance. Considering the popular rating of Peter Coddington it certainly was just as well that he had entered the works under some other name than his own.

But although the bitterness of this criticism rankled, its sting was removed by the thought that lazy and snobbish as Peter Coddington had been, thanks to Peter Strong he was neither lazy nor snobbish now; nor was he, the boy acknowledged, the disappointment to his father that he might have been had not prompt and heroic measures been taken. Yet even Peter Strong was obliged to admit after truthful scrutiny of his progress that there still was room for improvement. Accordingly he accepted submissively the censure that fell to his lot and, as Carmachel said, "did not consider himself the whole tannery just because one room in it was named after him."

It was not until the spring of that year that the next upward step came; then Peter and Nat were sent to the Elmwood plant for a few months' experience at the sole leather factories. The inconvenience of going seven miles and back every day was nothing to Peter because of his motorcycle; but for Nat the case was different. Poor Nat was dependent on street cars and once or twice, owing to delays, was tardy at the works. Then one morning the trolley broke down and Jackson was forced to walk three miles, arriving an hour late. In consequence his pay was docked. This injustice was too much for Peter. All day he thought about it.

"Father," he asked that evening when he arrived home, "do you think you would like to lend Peter Strong some money?"

"Lend money to Peter Strong! What for?"

Hotly, earnestly, eloquently, Peter presented his case concluding with the plea:

"Strong has some money in the bank, sir, but it is not enough. If he paid back what you lent him month by month do you think you could let him have what he needs to get a motorcycle for Nat?"

Mr. Coddington considered carefully.

"I do not at all approve of Peter Strong's borrowing money," said he. "It is a bad habit to fall into."

"But Peter Strong isn't going to make a habit of it, Father. And he isn't borrowing for himself, you know."

"Still he is borrowing."

"Yes, because if he waited until he had the cash in the bank Nat might be too old to ride a motorcycle," chuckled Peter, mischievously.

A quiet smile crept into the corners of Mr. Coddington's mouth.

"Well," admitted he deliberately, "the case does seem to be an urgent one. I might for once consent to break over my rule and furnish the sum necessary. Yet it is quite a large loan that Peter Strong is asking. I hope he will have no trouble in repaying it."

"I believe he can manage it all right," was the earnest reply. "His wages have been going up and will probably be raised still more in future. It does seem a little bit risky to loan him so much money, I confess, but I feel sure you will get it back if you are not in too much of a hurry for it."

Something in this answer evidently amused Mr. Coddington, for he bit his lip to keep back a smile and walked away to the window where he stood for some time looking out. At last he turned.

"We will close the deal, Peter," said he. "Since you vouch for Strong I will take a chance. I would advise you, though, to let me buy the motorcycle, as I can get a better price on it than you can."

"Thank you, Father."

Accordingly the dream that Peter had so long cherished really came true. The motorcycle was purchased, and the crate containing it was set down at the Jacksons' door the day before Easter.

Peter had planned not to say a word to Nat as to where it came from and therefore was not a little chagrined when both the members of the Jackson household jumped at once to the conclusion that the Coddington Company had sent it. Nat's mother, who, as Peter well knew, was a very proud woman, immediately refused to accept any more favors from that source and in consequence poor Peter was driven to confess his part in the mystery.

"But, Peter, my dear boy, you can't afford any such present as this. How have you the money to pay for so magnificent a gift to Nat? You, too, are working for your living and although you have no one dependent on you I am certain you do not possess a sufficient bank account to warrant your making such an extravagant purchase. It is like your big, kind, generous heart to want to do it, but of course Nat and I cannot let you take all your savings and give them away. How did you manage to get the motorcycle anyway?"

"I borrowed part of the money," explained Peter reluctantly.

"Oh, Peter, Peter! Borrowing is a dreadful habit! Never borrow money. You had much better go without almost anything than borrow money to get it."

"But I am paying up the loan week by week. My--the man I borrowed it from is making it very easy for me, and is in no hurry for the whole sum. You had better let me have my way, Mrs. Jackson. I am getting good wages and shall soon be earning even larger ones. I might blow in my spare cash on something dreadful--something much worse than a motorcycle," pleaded Peter, teasingly.

Nat's mother shook her head.

"I am not one bit afraid that you would."

"Oh, you never can tell," chuckled Peter. "Besides, can't you see that I shall have twice as much fun with my own motorcycle if Nat has one too? It is no earthly fun to go riding by myself."

This and many another such argument caused Mrs. Jackson to waver, and having once wavered her case was lost. Peter pursued his advantage and after a whole afternoon of reasoning succeeded in winning Nat's mother to his point of view. The motorcycle therefore was accepted in the spirit in which it was proffered and became Nat's most treasured possession.

What sport the two lads had going and coming from work! What wonderful Saturday afternoon rides they took through the surrounding country!

Their work at the sole leather tanneries was interesting, too. Here many new phases of leather making confronted them. First there was the tremendous weight of the great skins, which were so unwieldy that they could not easily be handled and, like cowhides, had to be cut into halves, or "sidees." In addition to this they were usually split--sometimes before tanning, sometimes after. The grain, or the side next the hair, was the more valuable leather. After being split once the splits could be split again, if desired, just as cowhides were. Some of the hides were tanned in oak bark, some in hemlock, and some in a mixture of both called union tannage.

Oak sole leather, the foreman said, was often considered preferable for soling shoes because its close fibre rendered it waterproof, and it seldom cracked. Much of the fine English leather imported into this country was, Peter learned, oak tanned. Since oaks grew so plentifully in Great Britain the bark was much less expensive there than here.

Hemlock leather--so deep red in color--was, on the other hand, used largely for heavy, stiff soles to common shoes for men and boys, since it made up in wear what it lacked in flexibility.

Union leather, being a combination of both oak and hemlock tannage, possessed the virtues as well as the faults of each; it had not the deep red of hemlock, nor the fine fibre of oak tanned leather. Still it was a flexible material and was used, the foreman told Peter, for soling women's shoes.

Sole leather seemed to the boys a very stiff and solid stuff after the calf and sheep skins which they had previously handled.

Perhaps they did not enjoy the Elmwood tanneries quite as much as the home works at Milburn, and perhaps they longed a little for their term of service there to be completed. Nevertheless they made friends, learned much that they were anxious to know, and had their motor rides over and back each day together.

With so many of his ambitions reaching fulfilment it began to seem to Peter as if life were a very smooth sea, and it was not until June when he and Nat were transferred to the patent leather factory that he had his first experience in navigating rough waters. This storminess came about through Tolman, a sharp-tongued foreman who did not hesitate to announce that too much favoritism had been shown Peter Strong in the past.

"I bet if he ever comes to the patent leather factory and I get the chance I will take some of the starch out of him," Tolman had been heard to declare.

Unluckily he held just enough authority to be able to carry out his threat. Power had hitherto been to him an unknown weapon. He had been given the position of acting foreman of the new patent leather factory only because of his long term of service with the company. It was understood that he was to hold the post until a skilled and competent foreman could be found; but while he enjoyed the distinction of "boss" he made as arrogant use of his sovereignty as he could.

From the first he blocked the way for Peter and Nat, not only by refusing to pass on to them any information, but by influencing the other men to follow his example. Whether he feared Peter Strong might usurp the vacant foremanship, or whether he simply cherished a grudge toward the lad because of his previous good fortune, it was impossible to discover. Whichever the case, his attitude was, from the moment the boys set foot in the new tannery, one of complete antagonism. Had it not been for Peter's agreement not to intrude his personal grievances at home it would have been easy to appeal to his father to straighten out the difficulty. But Peter would not for a moment consider this means of escape. Therefore he and Nat struggled on by themselves, picking up what scraps of information they were able. Try as they would they could wring from the workmen only the most meager facts about making patent leather.

They did succeed in finding out that the shiny varnish which gave it its finish was compounded in an isolated brick house in the factory yard where, after the ingredients had been carefully measured out, the mixture was boiled at a tremendous heat in great kettles. The formula for this dressing was a secret and was the result of many chemical experiments. All Peter and Nat could learn was that there was oil and Prussian blue in it, and something else with a stifling odor which caused it to dry quickly. No one was allowed in the room where, in the intense heat, the mixers--almost naked--toiled amid the clouds of steam which rose from the bubbling kettles. After the liquid had reached the necessary degree of temperature it was poured out into tanks where it was prevented from settling by being constantly agitated by the gentle motion of revolving paddles. Here it was kept until taken to the "slickers" to be used.

"And the reason that the building stands off by itself," declared Nat to Peter one day, "is because there is danger of the oil and stuff in the varnish taking fire or blowing up; I found that out from one of the men to-day. In that other low building off by itself are stored the supplies for making the varnish and that place has to be isolated too for the same reason."

"Good for you, Nat! We've gained one point anyhow. Did you find out anything else?"

"No. When the man saw that I was really interested he wouldn't tell me anything more. There is, though, a nice old Irishman--a friend of Carmachel's--here somewhere. I met him once at noon time over at the park. Maybe he will help us."

"There are plenty of things that I want to ask him if he ever turns up," Peter replied. "I only hope he will be decent to us. I am sure he would if he knew how hard we are trying to learn. One thing I am anxious to know is why on earth they don't dry the freshly varnished patent leather in the factory. Look at the work it makes for the men to bring it out here in the yard and stand it up against these hundreds of wooden racks. I should think by this time it would have dawned on somebody that it would be lots less trouble to dry it indoors in a hot room; shouldn't you?"

But it wasn't Nat who answered. Instead a voice with a decided Irish brogue replied kindly:

"Well, you see, my lad, no way has ever been found to dry patent leather except by the sun's rays. If somebody could invent a kind of japan that would dry in the house his fortune would be made. But nobody ever has. Every fine day the hundreds of frames have to be brought out and propped up in the sun--a jolly bit of work, I can tell you!"

"But suppose it should rain?" questioned Peter, eager to get all the information he could out of the friendly workman.

"If the weather is bad of course we do not put out the leather; in case a sudden storm comes up while it is out the factory whistle sounds and every man understands that he is to drop whatever he is doing, no matter what it is, and rush to the yard to help rescue the stock before it is spoiled."

"I never heard of anything so funny!" cried Peter.

"Funny, is it? You'll not be thinking so when you have to take your turn at it," protested the Irishman, grimly. "Just you be busy at doing some fussy thing you can't leave and wait till you hear the blast of the whistle! Out you'll have to cut and run like as if you were a schoolboy going through a fire drill. Then, you see, there are all those frames of wet leather to be set up somewhere indoors where they won't be injured until the storm is over and they can be carried out again."

"And suppose the stormy weather lasts several days?"

"No leather can be dried. Nor can you put it out on very dusty days lest the particles in the air stick on the moist surface and dry there. A strong wind is another bad thing, because it catches the frames as if they were sails and often smashes them all to pieces, spoiling the leather stretched on them."

"Well, it does seem as if somebody might be smart enough to think of some plan to prevent all this. Have people tried--lots of people, I mean--to make a gloss that will not need the sun to dry it?"

"Many and many a man has experimented and failed," replied the workman. "For years chemists have been working at the puzzle, but so far they never have got anywhere."

"If I only knew more about chemistry I'd try," cried Peter.

The old man looked amused at the boy's enthusiasm.

"Would you, indeed!" grinned he. "Well, if you succeeded you would be the first. But I'm not discouraging you, sonny. Sure if none of us were young and hopeful nothing great would be done in the world. You sound as if you might be Peter Strong--the lad they talk so much of in the other factories."

"I am Peter Strong."

"I might have guessed it! Carmachel said I'd know you because you had the strength of a tiger cub, the smile of the sun across the lake of Killarney, and the courage of a fighting cock. It's good to see you, laddie, starting out to move the world. I was going to do it once myself, but somehow I never did. It does no harm, though, to set out thinking you're going to budge the universe. Now listen to me. There is no kindly feeling toward you two boys in this place. Tolman is scared that you'll get his job away from him, so he's sore on your being sent here; the men are afraid of him so they side with him. Let me give you a bit of advice: work the best you can and have little to say to those around you. If you want to find out things keep your questions until you see me outside and I'll tell you all you want to know. I have been here twenty years, and what I can't answer I can ask. We'll beat Tolman yet, the three of us!"

And so to the kindly old McCarthy Peter and Nat entrusted their fortunes.

"I do believe we are going to like it at this factory, after all," announced Peter to Nat. "Certainly we shall not want for excitement. There is the chance to invent a better patent leather varnish which will dry indoors; there is the chance to learn the mystery of making patent leather despite Tolman; and there is the daily liability of having to tear out into the yard and rescue the stock from a sudden shower. It is going to be great sport, Nat!"

But Nat was not so sanguine.

Being a toggle-boy was far from easy work.

"And what is a toggle-boy?" inquired Mrs. Jackson at the end of their first day.

Peter and Nat only laughed.

They enjoyed using big words that mystified her.

"Why, you see, Mother, toggle-boys are what we are at present," said Nat, teasingly.

"But what does one have to do to be a toggle-boy?" persisted she.

"I am afraid a toggle-boy is not as grand a person as he sounds, Mrs. Jackson," interrupted Peter. "Nat and I are down at the lowest rung of the ladder again. We couldn't get much lower unless they set us to making the wooden frames the leather is stretched on before it is japanned. Somebody has to do that. The frames are about three yards long and two yards wide, roughly speaking; it isn't much work to make them, though, because the light thin boards come cut just the right size and simply have to be nailed together at the corners. Still I should not want to be set to doing carpentry. Even a toggle-boy's work is better than that--eh, Nat?"

"He is at least an inch nearer making leather," admitted Nat grudgingly.

"Of course he is! You see, Mrs. Jackson, Nat isn't stuck on his present job. I shouldn't be either if I expected to do it for life. It is not a position that inspires you with the feeling that you are well on your way toward being a captain of industry," Peter chuckled. "No, I'm afraid there is more than one step between being a toggle-boy and being president of the company."

Nat smiled in spite of himself.

"Now, Mrs. Jackson, to make our career a little clearer to you I'll tell you more about the toggle-boys," Peter continued. "When the dyed leather is sent over from the other factories to be made into patent leather it is first stretched on the wooden frames, as I told you, so that the gloss can be put on. The reason why they stretch the leather on frames instead of boards is because a frame, being open, allows the wet japan to run off the edges of the material and drip through to the floor as it could not do if it were stretched to a solid surface. They have found that for many reasons it is much better not to nail the leather to the frames. Nails make holes in the stock and waste it; besides the tacks might catch in the brushes as the men work and cause the dressing to spatter. Then, too, the leather is irregular in shape and some of it does not reach to the edges of the frame anyway. So steel nippers, or toggles, are snapped at intervals around the edge of the material and by means of strings knotted to the nippers the leather can be pulled out tightly and tied to the frame. Do you understand?"

Mrs. Jackson nodded.

"And you boys are the ones who put on the toggles?"

"Well, no, we're not," replied Peter, a little apologetically. "But we shall be some day. Just now we are employed in taking from the toggles that have already been used the strings that have been cut or knotted, and substituting instead new, long strings so that the nippers will be ready for the men."

"It isn't much of a job, Mother," put in Nat, ruefully.

"I admitted it was not next to the presidency," declared Peter, laughing. "But just keep in mind that we are not going to do it always."

And Peter's prediction was true, for in a few days notice came that the boys were to be promoted to a more difficult task.

Strangely enough, and fortunately too for the beginners, it was their cheery old friend McCarthy who gave them their first lesson in trimming off the stock to fit the frames; attaching the toggles, or nippers; and tying the leather so that every part of it could be drawn out taut.

"The finishers, or slickers as we call them, cannot put any gloss on unless the leather is perfectly tight," insisted McCarthy.

Peter tugged at his twine.

"What kind of stock do they use for patent leather?" he puffed. "Let me see! This must be----"

"Colt. Colt, calf, or kid is used. Colt, as you already know from your experience in the tanneries, is either the skin of a young horse or the split skin of a full-grown one. It works up into a light weight, fine grade patent leather. Calfskins you know all about too; they run light in weight anyway and, you remember, only need to be trimmed down to uniform thickness before tanning and dyeing. Patent calf is a heavy, air-tight leather which has been known to crack," whispered McCarthy with a wink, "but if it doesn't it wears well. Our best patent leather, though, is made from kid----"

"Which in reality is goat," interrupted Peter.

"True enough. So it is. Well, patent kid, as we call it, is not only light weight and elastic, but it is also porous. In fact, it is the only patent leather made that is not air-tight. It is the air-tightness of patent leather, you know, which makes it so hot to wear."

"Why, I always thought the trouble was with my feet!" ejaculated Peter.

McCarthy shook his head.

"Well, I never!" said Peter. "So it is the fault of the leather itself."

"I'm afraid it is, young one."

"Well, that settles it! I never shall buy another pair of patent leather shoes as long----"

"Go easy," retorted McCarthy dryly. "I guess you are safe, though, to make that vow. Your toggle-boy wages won't furnish you with endless numbers of patent leathers, I reckon. But cheer up! You won't be needing pumps here at the works, for while the richest of us always wear Tuxedos every day we excuse the small salary people from appearing in full dress."

Peter answered the jest with one of his well-known chuckles.

He was in high spirits, for although there was, as he himself was forced to own, many a step between him and the presidency of the Coddington Company he felt he had at least made one loyal friend in the patent leather factory-- McCarthy from the County of Cork!

When Saturday night came, however, and Peter received his pay envelope he peered anxiously inside it; then he drew a sigh of satisfaction.

"It is a lucky thing," he remarked to himself, "that Peter Strong is not on real toggle-boy wages. If he was he never would be able to pay the president another cent toward Nat's motorcycle!"

CHAPTER XI

TOLMAN EXPERIENCES A SHOCK

During the next few months Peter and Nat talked little and learned much. An occasional question was all they dared to ask, and that only when the men with whom they were associated seemed amiably disposed. Far from pushing their way to the front they took orders obediently from their superiors, slighting no task to which they were assigned, no matter how trivial it appeared. In consequence sentiment throughout the factory slowly turned in their favor. The chill silence of the workmen melted to gradual friendliness. Two such modest boys as these could not be coming to usurp anybody's position. No, indeed! First one and then another of the employees advanced bits of information which were accepted so gratefully that it became a pleasure to follow them with more. Before two months had passed the general opinion prevailed that Tolman had been grossly unjust to the newcomers, and with the reaction a strong desire arose among the men to atone for any previous unfairness.

This change in the atmosphere caused the good spirits which Peter and Nat had found it difficult to sustain through the ordeal of censure and misrepresentation to well up in a great happiness. Their daily work became a joy instead of a matter for dread. Making patent leather certainly was absorbingly interesting.

They had now reached the department where the varnish was put on the leather, and although not skilful enough to share in the actual doing the boys gained much knowledge simply by watching the process and asking questions. They learned that it was necessary to apply three coats of varnish to the material, and when the slickers put them on it was a fascinating operation. Sometimes the men used a rotary sweep of the arm, swirling the varnish round and round over the surface of the leather; sometimes they took quick backward and forward strokes. Usually four men worked together enameling a single skin. Amateurs would have spread the japan too thickly in some spots, too thinly in others; but not so these veterans at their trade. Deftly the blue-black liquid--so elastic and so oily--was coated over the leather, and the glistening finish put out in the sun to dry. After the second coat had hardened it was rubbed down with pumice that the surface might be perfectly smooth before the final layer of japan was applied. The last coat was then put on evenly with the spreaders of thin wood, and before the material was put out for its last sunning it was baked in an oven heated to a temperature of about a hundred and sixty degrees.

"I should think the last baking would be enough to dry the stuff without putting it outdoors a third time," ventured Peter to one of the men.

"Wouldn't you!" responded the laborer with a smile. "But no! Nothing but the sun will do the business."

"It's strange, isn't it?" mused Peter.

"Strange, and almighty inconvenient," his companion assented.

That it was inconvenient Peter, after his months of experience at the factory, agreed only too cordially. Many a shower had fallen and more than once had he been forced to rush out into the yard at the sound of the whistle and help the others drag the half dry stock to a place of shelter. Since the difficulty was one not to be obviated it was accepted good-humoredly as an evil necessary to this branch of leather manufacture.

"I tell you what, Nat, some day science has got to find a way to get rid of certain obstacles that stand in the path of making leather," declared Peter. "Somebody must invent an unhairing device to do away with the taking off of the white hair by hand. You'd better try your brain at the puzzle. Another chance for you to make yourself famous is to think out a machine for softening fine leather that will take the place of knee-staking. Still another opportunity to write your name in golden letters across the tanneries of the world is to perfect a patent leather varnish that will dry indoors. Now there are three roads to fortune open to you, old man. You'd better select one."

Nat grinned.

"After you, Peter," said he. "You choose your path to fame first and I will follow."

"I'll leave the fame to you, Nat," laughed Peter. "Somehow I've never aspired to be famous--it's lucky for me, I guess, that I haven't, too."

But fame came to Peter notwithstanding--came that very day, and in a way he did not at all expect.

Directly after lunch he was sent by Mr. Tolman to the office in Factory 1 to carry some samples of finished leather to Mr. Tyler. Little dreaming how eventful was to be his errand he set out, whistling as he went. Mr. Tyler was busy that afternoon, so busy that he glanced hurriedly at the samples of stock, gave Peter a roughly scrawled message to take back, and dismissed him. Now it happened that the patent leather plant was quite a little walk from the other factories, for the site purchased for it was far less convenient than the old ball field would have been. A dusty stretch of road intervened which wound its way to the summit of a rise of ground and then sloped gradually down to the yard of the new factory. Peter ambled up this hill none too swiftly, for the day was hot, and on reaching its crest he was surprised to notice that although the sun was shining brightly overhead across the green marshes to the east a shower was stealing in from the distant sea.

Instantly his mind flew to the tannery. The patent leather would have to be rushed in. To-day an unusually large quantity of stock was sunning on the racks, and it would take the united efforts of all hands to get it under cover before the approaching storm reached the factory yards.

Even now the warning whistle should be sounding.

Peter stood still and listened.

But no discordant blast broke the stillness.

He quickened his steps.

Despite the cloudless blue of the heavens the wall of mist with its burden of rain was steadily creeping nearer.

There must be some mistake.

Tolman couldn't have seen the storm coming.

Breaking into a run Peter dashed in at the factory gate and raced up two stairs at a time to the office.

Tolman was nowhere to be seen. The room was empty!

Aghast, the boy glanced about. Every second was precious. What should he do? He thought a moment of his father and what the loss would mean to the company. Then, without further hesitation, he touched the bell that gave to the engineer the signal for the blowing of the factory whistle.

It seemed as if the interval of silence in which Peter waited, listening only to the beating of his own heart, was endless.

Then the well-known belch from the great chimney told him that his warning was being carried to every corner of the building. From the window he could see the men, hatless and alert, pouring out into the yard.

Eager to join in the work he rushed down-stairs and was soon in the thick of the excitement.

Although the sun was still unclouded no one questioned the wisdom of the order. In and out toiled the men and the stock was very nearly all within doors when Mr. Tolman strode into the yard.

His face was flushed with rage.

"Who gave that signal?" he bawled when he came near enough to be heard.

Every one stopped.

Immovable with surprise the men waited, the great frames of wet leather suspended in their hands.

Peter Strong stepped forward.

"I did, Mr. Tolman," he answered quietly.

"How dare you touch that bell! I'll teach you, young man, that we have no practical jokes here."

"It isn't a joke," Peter said. "I tried to find you and tell you that a storm was coming. When I couldn't, I gave the signal myself."

"Who's running this factory, Strong--you or I? Tell me that."

"You wouldn't want the stock ruined, Mr. Tolman."

"That's my affair. Storm! There isn't going to be any storm! You're a meddlesome young scoundrel! Just because you have had some notice taken of you over at the other works you think you can come in here and run the whole place. Well, I'll show you that you can't manage my business."

Fuming with anger Tolman sprang forward, his arm upraised.

"Don't you touch that boy, Tolman!" cried a voice from the crowd.

It was McCarthy.

But the man was too enraged to heed the warning.

With a quick thrust he struck out toward the lad.

All the blood in Peter's body seemed to throb in his cheeks. Swiftly as a deer he leaped forward and, catching the upraised arm, he held it as if in a vise.

"Let me go! Let me go, or it will be the worse for you," blustered Tolman, struggling vainly to wrench himself free from Peter's grasp.

"I shall not let you go until you cool down a bit, Mr. Tolman," replied Peter firmly.

"You had no right to meddle," snapped Tolman.

"I had the same right that any man has to prevent the destruction of the company's property," was Peter's retort.

"You let me go this minute, you young cub, or you'll regret it," yelled Tolman in a fury. "Who are you that you think you can come here and give orders to me and my men?"

Fearlessly Peter met his eye. Then he sent the man spinning into the crowd.

"Who am I, Mr. Tolman? Who am I? I'll answer that question. I am Peter Coddington, and I have the right to protect my father's property whenever I think it is necessary."

An awed silence fell upon the group of men.

[Illustration: HE SENT THE MAN SPINNING INTO THE CROWD]

No one doubted the truth of the lad's assertion. It spoke in the dignity of his whole figure; in the proud poise of his head; in the unflinching gaze with which he met their eyes.

Of course he was Peter Coddington!

Why had they never guessed it before?

More than one man, as the work of carrying in the skins was completed, reviewed in his mind Peter's career at the tanneries and marveled that he had not suspected the secret from the first.

Tolman, astounded at the shock of the discovery, paused, then shuffled shamefacedly forward as if to offer an apology, but no word came to his lips.

The awkwardness of the stillness was dispelled by Peter himself, who, turning at last to the men, said simply: "We made good time getting the leather under cover, and we were none too soon. See--here comes the rain!"

* * * * *

How the news sped through the vast tanneries! It seemed fairly to leap from one building to another. On every hand the men took up the tale and discussed it.

Peter Strong--their Peter--was the president's son! He was Peter Coddington!

It was all too wonderful to believe; and yet, after all, it was so simple!

Why hadn't they known it all along, the workmen asked each other.

"He was a thoroughbred from the minute he began pitching calfskins!" ejaculated Carmachel. "Think of it! Think of his pitching calfskins in my old brown overalls--him as could have picked out any job in the tannery that he chose!"

"And think of the months he put in working in the beamhouses too! Slaving away there in the smell and heat just like any of the rest of us!" said another man.

"And how he duffed in in the other department! He wasn't afraid of getting his hands dirty! And what a worker he was!"

"And mind how he stood by us men and got the park for us--stood up and faced his father man to man. The Little Giant!"

"Aye! Don't forget the ball playing!"

"And how he brought his lunch every day like the rest of us!"

On every hand the men admitted that their idol, Peter, was indeed worthy to be the son of the president of the great Coddington tanneries.

"And yet I can't help thinking," reflected Carmachel, "that in spite of his parentage, and his money, and everything else he really is our Peter--a product of the works, just as his father said."

There was little work done in the factories that afternoon. Excitement ran too high. Over and over the men talked in undertones of the wonderful story. Of course no one questioned its veracity and yet there was no rest until the tale was taken to Mr. Coddington for confirmation. It was Tyler who first ventured to broach the matter to the president. He related the chain of events leading up to Peter's avowal and then, receiving no reply, fumbled uncomfortably at his scarf-pin and wished he had not spoken.

Finally Mr. Coddington glanced up, answering with characteristic terseness:

"Yes, it is true that Peter is my boy, Tyler," he said. "Not a bad sort either, as boys go."

"Why, he is one boy in a hundred, Mr. Coddington--a son to be proud of!" burst out Tyler.

"Oh, Peter has possibilities," admitted the president with a smile.

But he would say nothing more. Instead he shut himself up in his office where he went determinedly to work. But those who peeped through the glass door could see that throughout the whole afternoon the smile that had lighted his face still lingered there faintly.

He smiled as he rode home in his big limousine too, and he continued to smile during dinner, but he said nothing.

Peter, who was watching him closely, thought every instant he would either make some allusion to the events of the day or make some opening so that he could do so.

Now that all was over the boy was not a little chagrined that in a moment of anger he should have let his secret pass his lips. Henceforth the game was spoiled. Probably his father thought he should not have lost his temper and blurted out the truth. It was a foolish thing to do and now that he thought it over coolly Peter regretted that he had done it. He longed to talk with his father, but he did not just know how to begin.

He was finally spared the embarrassment of confession or explanation, for as the president pushed back his chair from the table he remarked casually:

"So your secret is out, son."

"Yes, sir. I didn't mean to tell, but I got so angry at Tolman, Father."

"Well, perhaps it is just as well to travel under your own name from now on. It's a rather good name. And by the by, Peter, here is a receipt for the money Strong owes me on that motorcycle. We'll cancel that debt. The company was saved several times the amount by getting that lot of patent leather in out of the rain to-day."

"But I can't take money for that, Father," stammered Peter.

"Strong can. That will close my dealings with him. To me it is worth a far bigger sum than that to get my own boy back again."

CHAPTER XII

MR. CODDINGTON TELLS A STORY

One of the first things Peter did the next afternoon was to go with his father and mother to Mrs. Jackson's and relate to her himself all the happenings of the previous day. The story was, to be sure, no surprise to her, for had not Nat rushed home and incoherently rattled it off? But how much nicer it was to hear it from Peter! The boy spared no detail of the truth; he told of his school, his failures there, of his disgust at being put into the tanneries, of his desire to conceal his identity. During the tale no one interrupted him. Mr. and Mrs. Coddington, Mrs. Jackson, and Nat all listened intently to the end. Then when the story was at last finished Peter looked up and smiled at Nat's mother.

"So one of your sons, you see, has been sailing under a false name, Mrs. Jackson," he concluded whimsically. "Do you think you can forgive him?"

"You must try," pleaded Mr. Coddington, putting in a laughing word. "My son has been doing the same thing and yet I've overlooked it."

Everybody smiled and the tension was instantly broken.

"But to think neither Nat nor I ever suspected you, Peter!" mused Mrs. Jackson. "We must have been very stupid. Why, I don't see how we could have helped guessing the truth long ago. As I look back on it all it seems as if a score of incidents might have told us. Either you kept your secret marvelously well or Nat and I are not very keen."

"And even though you fooled every one else, Peter, I can't quite understand how you fooled me," murmured Nat.

"Peter certainly carried his scheme through well," declared Mrs. Coddington. "Yet for our part we are very glad that the time for dissembling is past."

"Indeed we are," Mr. Coddington echoed. "This game of Peter's has complicated our plans to no small extent."

"Why, Father, I did not know it made any difference to anybody except myself," Peter answered, looking at his parents in surprise.

"Nevertheless it has made a difference, my son," returned the president of the company kindly. "Strong was assuredly a good fellow; indeed he was a lad to whom I always shall feel grateful, for he has taught me several lessons that I needed to learn."

Peter opened his eyes very wide.

To think of his father's learning lessons!

"Still," continued Mr. Coddington, "so long as Peter Strong and not Peter Coddington formed a part of our household many plans which we had hoped to make realities had to be abandoned. Now, however, we shall try to carry through some of them; one in particular we are eager to see fulfilled, and that is why Mrs. Coddington and I have come here to-day."

Peter wondered what was coming.

His mother answered the question that trembled on his lips.

"Your father and I thought best not to tell you beforehand, Peter," she said softly.

"I'll do it, whatever it is, Father," cried Peter. "Only please do not say that you want me to go back to school. I'd even do that, though, if you really thought I had better," he added bravely.

Mr. Coddington dropped his hand on the boy's shoulder and smiled down into the anxious face.

"There will be no more school for you, son," he answered slowly. "At least not the sort of school that you dread so much. No, in future you must find your books in the great world about you--in men, and in the things they are doing; and this education of yours is precisely the subject I came here to talk about."

Leaning forward the president began slowly:

"Mrs. Jackson, on the fifteenth of next month, Mrs. Coddington and I are to sail for England."

"What!" gasped Peter, forgetting for the moment that he should not interrupt.

"We are to take Peter with us," went on Mr. Coddington ignoring the interruption and proceeding in the same earnest, deliberate tone. "He has worked hard and faithfully, and needs a good rest. The trip, however, is not to be an entirely profitless one, for while in England I shall take him to visit some of the finest tanneries, that he may observe other methods for doing the same things that we are doing here."

An exclamation of pleasure escaped Peter's lips.

His father smiled.

"After we have collected in England all the information possible and have seen something of the sheep country there, and the great houses from which hides are shipped, we shall go to Paris and place orders for several large consignments of skins. I want my son to see for himself, Mrs. Jackson, just how this end of the business is conducted, for I hope and expect that some day these duties will be his, and I want him equipped to meet them with wisdom and intelligence."

"You mean that you are going to fit Peter to manage the tanneries," nodded Mrs. Jackson.

"Precisely."

There was a pause.

No one spoke.

It was evident that Mr. Coddington had more to say, and that he was finding it a little difficult to continue.

"In this great business, however," he went on at last, "Peter will need help. He will not be able to carry so much care all alone."

"But you will----" burst out Peter.

"Oh, I shall be around here for some time yet, God willing," replied his father cheerily. "Still we old fellows cannot expect to stay here forever. We must consider the future, dear boy. Therefore I wish to train up another lad to share Peter's burdens with him--a fellow with good stuff in him; some one whom Peter likes and can trust. It is with this end in view, Mrs. Jackson, that when we sail for England we wish to take your son with us."

"Me!"

Nat sprang from his chair.

"Would you like to go, Nat?" asked Mrs. Coddington, watching the light leap into the boy's eyes.

"Would I like to go! Why, it is the thing I have dreamed of all my life--dreamed of, and never expected to be able to do. To go to Europe! To see all those places I've read about and seen pictures of! Think of it! Do you really mean it, Mr. Coddington?"

"I certainly do, my boy," answered the president, heartily enjoying his delight. "I cannot promise to take you to all your dream-countries but you shall see some of them. It all rests with your mother. If she gives her consent you shall go."

Mrs. Jackson's answer was ready. While Mr. Coddington had been speaking she, with woman's intuition, had leaped forward to the coming question and had decided upon her reply. Her one thought was for her boy. She did not permit a consideration of self to bar his way.

"I am only too glad to give my consent, Mr. Coddington," she said firmly. "It is a great opportunity for Nat, and his mother would be the last person to allow him to refuse it. Of course he shall go."

Then the significance of her words broke upon Nat.

He flushed.

He was mortified to realize that in his enthusiasm his thought had been only for himself and his own pleasure. For an instant his face fell. Then he sprang to his mother's side and throwing his arms about her exclaimed:

"Of course I shall not go, mother. Go, and leave you here all by yourself! I guess not! I did not think at first that my going would mean that. It was very good of you, Mr. Coddington, to ask me, but nothing would hire me, sir, to leave my mother."

"Oh, you would not be leaving me for long, dear," argued his mother, crushing the boy's cheek against her own and hurriedly dashing away a tear. "Why, people go back and forth across the ocean every day. It is not--not far--very far.

You could write to me often and before you or I knew it you would be back at home again." The trembling voice gained steadiness. "Why, it would be nothing at all, Nat! And think of all the stories you would have to tell me! While you were away I could get books and read about the places you were seeing and----"

"I never shall leave you here alone, mother, never!" repeated Nat.

"But we do not mean to have you leave your mother, Nat dear," Mrs. Coddington said. "You have not waited to hear the end of our plan. Your mother is to go too. She is to be my guest on the trip. Oh, yes, Mrs. Jackson. That is the other part of our plan. I shall be very forlorn while these three leather makers are rushing about among the tanneries and warehouses. They won't want to take me with them--nor am I at all sure I should care to go if they did. So I am depending for my pleasure on your companionship, you see."

With charming grace she bent forward and put her hand pleadingly on Mrs. Jackson's.

"You won't refuse Peter's mother this favor, will you?" she begged.

Mrs. Jackson covered the hand with her own slender one and when she answered her voice quivered with emotion.

"You are very, very kind, both you and Mr. Coddington," she answered. "I have no words to thank you; but believe me, while I heartily appreciate your generosity, I feel that too much has already been done for Nat and me--far more than I should have accepted had I realized that it was Mr. Coddington himself and not the company who was doing it. Do not consider me ungracious in being unwilling to add this favor to the others. I would rather be under obligations to you and Mr. Coddington than to any one else in the world if it were possible. Nat shall go. The trip will be a wonderful education for him and he will, I am sure, work hard in the future to repay you for your kindness; but I could not accept such a gift."

Unconsciously Mrs. Jackson's chin lifted, and her figure drew itself up.

"Oh, but *I* want you to go," broke in Peter.

Smiling, she shook her head.

"I think, if you will pardon my frankness, you are making too much of a very slight thing, Mrs. Jackson," declared Mr. Coddington. "Come, be honest. You are too proud to accept this trip from Mrs. Coddington and me. Isn't that it? You doubt her wanting you as a traveling companion. But there you wrong her. She really does want you. It would be a genuine favor to her, and the obligation would be entirely on our side, you see."

"I think your kindness blinds you to your real motive, Mr. Coddington," Mrs. Jackson returned.

"Then listen. I will tell you a story. Long ago, at the time of the Civil War, my father----" Mrs. Jackson started, then recovered herself; but there was no question that his words had caught her keenest attention.

Imperturbably he went on with his tale.

"My father, who was a fearless young Northerner, was sent forward to carry a dispatch through the Southern lines. It was a dangerous mission and on the delivery of that message depended not alone his honor but a large measure of the success of the Northern cause. He pledged his life to carry that word. All went well until quite without warning he found himself in a rebel ambush. He made his escape but in so doing was seriously wounded and nothing but the speed of his horse prevented his recapture. His enemies were still hot in pursuit when he found he could go no further. Then when he saw his strength failing and knew the struggle was useless he took a desperate chance. A plantation stood in his path and he rode up to the house and begged for aid. Now it happened that the owners of that plantation, although Southerners, were in sympathy with the Northern cause; not only did they take in the wounded man and nurse him back to life, but the son of the family, a daring lad, ventured to continue the ride through the lines and deliver the stranger's message."

Mr. Coddington paused a moment.

"And did he succeed?" cried Peter breathlessly.

"Yes."

"Oh, it was splendid! Think of a boy's doing a thing like that for his country!"

"And a boy not much older than you either, Peter," added Mrs. Jackson eagerly.

"Why--why--how did you know?" queried Peter, bewildered.

Instantly Mrs. Jackson was all confusion; but she did not explain her impulsive words.

"That Northern soldier, Peter, was your grandfather," declared Mr. Coddington quickly. "He all but died in the fulfilment of his task and had it not been for the nursing he received in that Southern home he undoubtedly would have done so. His family owed his life, his honor, and the success of the cause they prized so dearly to those brave friends who risked everything they possessed to serve their country and a fellow creature. And now if you will ask Mrs. Jackson perhaps she can tell you who the boy was who carried the dispatch through the Southern lines."

"It was my brother--Nat's uncle, Peter," whispered Mrs. Jackson.

"Why, mother," Nat ejaculated, "you never told me it was these Coddingtons!"

"And not until the day I came to see you at the hospital, Nat, did I find out that it was these Jacksons," said Mr. Coddington. Then turning to Nat's mother he said: "Now you must certainly admit that the Coddingtons, Mrs. Jackson, owe a good deal to the Jacksons--life, honor, their country's success. Between your family and mine on which side lies the obligation?"

"It was a service gladly rendered."

"But one that cost your family dear. Oh, I have discovered, you see, how the incident came to the knowledge of your Southern neighbors and how, in rage, they burned your father's plantation driving you all from it. I have looked up all the facts. Your father came North in the hope of recovering his fortunes; he died; you married, strangely enough, another Jackson; your husband was unfortunate and before he won a place in life he, too, was taken from you and you were left with this boy. You strayed into Milburn--it is needless to go on; you see I know all your story. I wished, my dear madam, to verify my suspicions. I have verified them. You and Nat unconsciously came to a haven where you never again shall have cause to worry. Your son shall be trained to share my son's fortunes. The Coddingtons can never cancel their debt to the Jacksons, but at least they shall repay a part of it. You who know so well what pride is will not, I am sure, deny me this pleasure and satisfaction."

For a few moments there was silence.

Then Mrs. Jackson extended her hand toward Mr. Coddington.

"Let us not consider it a debt between strangers," she said. "Rather let it be a bond between friends. I will gladly accept your kindness and go to England with you all."

* * * * *

And so two weeks later Peter, amid the cheers of the workmen, bade good-bye to the tanneries.

As he and his father stood alone on the deck of the great liner and watched her make her way out of the harbor Mr. Coddington said:

"Do you recall, Peter, the evening of your failure at school, and how I told you that although it was hard for me to be so severe I felt I must make a man of you?"

"Yes, sir."

"I was very confident in my own strength that night; but I see now I was not so powerful as I thought, and it is you who have shown me my folly. No one in this world can build the character of another; each of us must rear his own. You have made a far better man of yourself, my boy, than I ever could have made of you. I am proud of my son, Peter!"

* * * * *

THE END

www.ingramcontent.com/pod-product-compliance
Lightning Source LLC
Chambersburg PA
CBHW060416290526
45791CB00002B/770